The Wake of the Cachalots

SIMON DANIELS

First Edition published 1992 by Simon Daniels

Copyright © Simon Daniels 1992.

All rights reserved. No part of this book may be reproduced, stored in a retrieval system or transmitted, in any form or by whatever means, without the prior permission in writing of the Publisher, nor be otherwise circulated in any form of binding or cover other than that in which it is published and without a similar condition including this condition being imposed on the subsequent purchaser.

ISBN 0 9519217 0 3

6 The Mews
Red Lodge
Chandler's Ford
Eastleigh
Hampshire
SO5 3SF
U.K.

THE WAKE OF THE CACHALOTS

Master Mariners of an Island Race

Contents

To Glory We Steer	1
John Moffat: A Cadet's Adventures	9
Jack Holt – Pilot of the Superliners	35
Norman Lucas – Scenes from British India	45
Watts Watts – Tramping with the Boatsteerer	71
Gordon Renshawe and 'The Navvics'	79
Ron Freaker: Blue Stars, Blue Whales	87
A Tribute to Commodore MacLean	107
Ocean Express – Reg Kelso and the Union Castle Line	117
Richard Whistler – The Cachalots sail on	137
John Noble: Going Ashore	143
'Finished With Engines'	155

Cover photograph: Captain Richard Whistler

TO GLORY WE STEER

One of the obvious reasons for having a war is to make your country richer. No doubt Napoleon thought so too, which was a good joke on him because the effect of the Napoleonic Wars was to enrich France's oldest enemy. For Britain, the long wars with France that ended in 1815 had created a demand for all kinds of manufactured goods, while at the same time they conveniently disabled European competition. Britain had been the supplier of almost everything to the allied armies, with the result that these wartime dealings had hugely increased the experience of British businessmen in international trade. The profits which were earned increased the amount of capital in Britain available for investment in industry, so that more investment enabled industry to expand, so more dividends were paid, so more money was invested again.

It was a very short time before this expansion was taken to the Empire, to where machinery, expertise and optimistic emigrants were exported and their lucrative products imported. There was only one way to convey it all: by sea. This meant that the fortunes of a businessman in the shipping industry would improve tremendously. The main problem was time: the only motive power for ships was by sail. If you wanted to send a letter to a station in the Australian outback, it could be eighteen months before you received a reply. Let us take the example of Australia a little further, to see the transition from sail to steam. The oldest shipping company trading there from the UK was the Aberdeen Line, whose magnificent clippers were consistently the first to reach British ports with the new season's wool and the company's owner George Thompson had not felt it necessary to purchase his first steamship until 1881. By then steam was the reality for the future, though and in 1881 the company's first steamer, the *Aberdeen*, was launched, the same year in which the company's famous *Thermopylae* made her last voyage to China.

The idea of steam propulsion was not new but it was a slow starter. In 1784 an American named John Fitch discussed the possibility of vessels driven by steam, but the reactions were sideways glances with deep suspicions about his sanity. He raised enough capital to develop a mechanical oar and although he appreciated the properties of steam he was wrong about the mechanism. It was not until 1812 that a little steamer named the *Comet* plied up and down the Clyde. Commanding only four horsepower, nevertheless she was the foundation stone upon which the Industrial Revolution was able to build the mighty steamship and satisfy the needs of business. Early vessels were all paddle steamers but in 1845 the British Admiralty tested a screw-driven sloop against a paddle steamer similar in size and power. The test consisted of a tug of war with the ships lashed stern to stern. The screw-driven ship won on a spectacular scale, towing the paddle steamer backwards.

The screw was a boon to the shipping business: screw-driven vessels burned a quarter of the coal consumed by paddle steamers so they were less expensive to run because less coal had to be purchased and less time was wasted bunkering for fewer coaling stops were needed. This is important because during bunkering obviously a ship is not going any where so she is not earning any money. The crew's wages still have to be paid, though. Moreover, screws could take between twice and three times as much cargo and even more times as many passengers. At the same time, timber hulls had reached their maximum size, for they could not take the stresses involved in higher gross tonnage aswell as the stresses on the hull arising out of the motion of screw propulsion. Technology came to the rescue with the iron hull dashing the limitations (and maintenance costs) of timber hulls.

The scene was set for the greatest leap forward in maritime history – and it was also the cue for an ancient port on England's south coast to rise from obscurity to world prominence.

Southampton has always had natural advantages which place it far ahead of its rivals. Lying mid-way in the English Channel the port is open to the sea yet has the shelter of its position at the top of Southampton Water. Southampton's tides are unique and justly famous. Over a tidal cycle of 12.4 hours the tide is either rising or standing at high water for 8.5 of those hours. The phenomenon of double high water lasts two hours on each tide. If the English Channel is imagined as a rectangular tank 300 nautical miles long, 36 fathoms deep and pivoted at its mid-length, when tipped towards one end the water flows towards that end. Thus when it is high water at Dover it is low water at Lands End; at the centre the level remains **constant**. The effect of the sun and moon relative to the earth creates this effect precisely, which is called oscillation and occurs twice daily. There is another effect: the friction, irregular depths and restriction in width of the English Channel result in a further four oscillations daily which produces the double high water in the port. All unique assets, but in those early days expansion of Southampton as a port could not be expected unless there were reasonable communications with London. Remember that at this time, the only transport to the Metropolis was by road. A modern-day cart track is a fair image of a major trunk road in the early nineteenth century: dusty as hell and pock-marked with huge pot-holes in the summer, with a transformation in winter to a muddy quagmire. People were not going to use a port unless they could get away from it, to their destination, which mainly would be the Capital. The commercial need for speedier communication was vital.

The Industrial Revolution produced the solution, and in 1834 an Act was passed to form the London and Southampton Railway Company. Completed in 1840, its effect reduced a journey of two days to at most a few hours. With its greatly improved communications with the business centre of London and with its geographical advantages and double high tides, businessmen saw spectacular opportunities in this fascinating maritime town, which remains fascinating today despite interferance from Adolph Hitler. With construction of the railway in progress, in 1836 an Act of Parliament was passed for the formation of the Southampton Dock Company. The foundation stone of the docks was laid with full masonic honours on the 23rd October 1838 by the Grand Master for Hampshire and the docks were opened on the 29th August 1843.

By 1853 when Queen Victoria reviewed her fleet at Spithead, the port was already becoming the premier passenger port of Britain, now the workshop of the world. P and O's pioneering steamers sailed from Southampton from the outset, as did those of the Royal Mail Steam Packet Company. The British Empire was founded on Commerce and Sea Power, embodied by the merchant marine protected by the Royal Navy and the nineteenth century saw the port grow with our merchant service, but for Southampton the Toll of the Sea was no hackneyed cliché, as the monuments around the city and its cemeteries testify today. One particular memorial recalls the crews of three steamers of the Royal Mail Steam Packet Company which foundered with heavy loss of life in just one hurricane at St Thomas on the 29th October 1867.

Today, we read about those epoch-making days in the comfortably sanitised, pious history books that deal magnificently with statesmen and battles and lines on maps, but how much has been recorded of the men at the sharp end of the proceedings? Only in forgotten letters, long left to dust, can we read, almost with incredulity, about the everyday lives of those men who made the Empire work, when the ships' masters were as responsible for bargaining for the cargoes in foreign parts as they were for the safe custody of their ships. Ian Thomson, Captain of the Southampton Master Mariners' Club in 1991, treasures a collection of letters from his great grandfather, Captain Robert Thomson, who commanded the China tea clipper *Scawfell* in the 1860's. Everyday news takes on a fascination for us, striking a new shaft of sunlight onto our appreciation of the times, as we read in a letter which Captain Thomson wrote to his wife from the *Scawfell* while docked at Shanghai in June 1863:

> "We have been getting on very slow with the loading, the price of tea being so high that the merchants cannot buy it; the Whinfell had to be sent to Foo-Chow eight days ago, they being unable to load us both here, there are none of the ships here getting away so early as expected and in consequence of there being so many ships here and the teas so high in price the freights [rates] have come down, we are now loading at £5 10/- instead of £6 10/- expected when I came here besides being longer in getting away we are more likely to make a long passage down the China Sea, so that you need not expect me so soon as last year.

To Glory We Steer

"The *Chauzee* sails today he is not quite full but he will not wait any longer he is in such a hurry to get first home, the *Crulnakyle* Capt Morrison sailed yesterday, the *Gunnivere* and *Glen-Aros* will be next and probably after that your humble servant...."

Ten days later he wrote:

"The last of our cargo is now alongside and we sail today about 11 o'clock. I am not sure of getting clear of the river today as the winds are right ahead outside, the South West Monsoon being blowing strong. Now I must say goodbye until you hear from me again from the Downs which I hope will not be more than four months."

By the turn of the century, marine technology had made it much safer to conduct business in great waters and at last Samuel Johnson's description of going to sea – like going to prison with the chance of being drowned – became no more than a joke. Perhaps too much of a joke, for the Seas have never ceased to punish Man whenever he becomes too complacent of their powers.

In 1907 the White Star Line's *Adriatic* docked in Southampton, heralding the start of the port's pre-eminence in the Atlantic Ferry business and the association with one of the most evocative names in maritime transport: White Star, which by that time was owned by the American combine International Mercantile Marine.

All too soon came the merchant service's severe test in the Great War when devestating losses were suffered. Southampton's master mariners were called upon to turn their vessels to duties of trooping, or to feeding hungry Britons with fast reefer ships, or to operating as armed merchant cruisers; but perhaps the most poignant memory for Southampton people would remain the sight of ocean liners, so glamorous in peacetime, now converted into hospital ships, sailing into the docks packed with wounded friend and foe still caked in Flanders mud, bound for the great Royal Victoria Hospital at Netley.

By the time that Cunard moved its express passenger service to Southampton in 1919 with the *Mauretania* and *Aquitania*, the port was already gearing up for the massive post-war boom in trade that came to epitomise the glamour of express ocean travel. Ocean leviathans that became household names were seen in the port virtually daily and in the summer of 1928 White Star, back in British hands, placed an order with Harland and Wolff for the construction of a new express liner, the *Oceanic*, to continue to maintain the tradition and position of the White Star Line in the North Atlantic trade.

It was not just the Atlantic Ferry that was flourishing in Southampton; many companies were using the port as the UK base for services to the farthest parts of the world, like the Aberdeen and Commonwealth Line to Australia, the old Aberdeen Line whom we met earlier, that moved here in 1928. By this time, the masters of the ships using Southampton, be they mighty liners or hungry tramps, had seen *everything*. Many of them had started their service in sailing ships and were seasoned Cape Horners. They had limited time in port but there was no place where they could gather and relax among kindred spirits: what they wanted was a club of their own. So it was, that on the 15th February 1928 seventeen master mariners met in a room at the offices of the Royal Mail Steam Packet Company in Southampton. Captain A H Raymer, RD, opened the meeting to ascertain whether a club was desirable. They agreed unanimously to band together to form a club and thus was born the Southampton Master Mariners' Club, whose master-members have always embraced the title 'Cachalots', a species of whale that has the thickest skin, blows the hardest and spouts the most!

The club swiftly became extremely popular, attracting many respected names in White Star, Union-Castle, Royal Mail and other companies, not to mention Cunard of course, including Arthur Rostron, the master of the *Carpathia* which raced 58 miles to the foundering *Titanic* in 1912. The youngest member of the club was Bruce Bell, of Highfield Crescent, Southampton, a true Southampton boy who went to King Edward VI School. Bruce was one of the last mariners to gain a square-rigged master's certificate and gained much experience under sail before his service in the Strick Line, a distinguished company in which Douglas Gates would serve many years later. Douglas is a truly substantial figure in the club today and in its 60th Jubilee Year he was elected a harpooner, or committee-member.

Donald MacLean concluded in the club's first history:

> "In keeping with other progressive organisations, the Master Mariners' Club has kept in step with the times, perhaps conservatively, but bearing in mind the Chinese proverb, 'It is a wise bamboo that bends with the wind.' "

Wise, indeed, for by the club's sixtieth anniversary year the British deep sea merchant fleet had all but disappeared and for the surviving nucleus, life at sea today is a serious matter of high technology and business management spiced with a nagging worry about offending against the 1988 Merchant Shipping Act. With our future to be found in the new, united Europe metamorphosing from East to West, we have new horizons to look forward to – but, like all the European cultures, we should also look back at those people in our own history who made us great. Many of them are not too long past, some of them are still with us. It would be wrong to call them a dying breed, though: the blood of the British contains a fair amount of salt water and seafaring is what we do best, be it in a square rigged sailing ship from a bygone era or an open-hatch container ship of the 1990's. So it is right that we should reckon up the value of the Cachalots of the Red Duster, the one industry which, as an island race, guaranteed our survival. But how can we go about this Reckoning Up?

Best ask the Cachalots themselves.

The Wake of the Cachalots

JOHN MOFFAT:
A CADET'S ADVENTURES

John Moffat saw distinguished service for many years as a master with the Royal Fleet Auxiliary, but his formative years were spent learning the business of seafaring with the Clan Line. Here he recalls his adventures as a cadet in a way of life that has largely passed into history.

In 1943 I was approaching my fifteenth birthday and had long decided that I wanted to join the Merchant Navy as a deck cadet and hopefully be successful in eventually reaching that great, exalted position of Master of a North Atlantic liner. Quite a number of seafarers who had suffered unemployment during the Depression in the 'thirties, advised me against following a career at sea. I am glad to say that I did not accept their advice: I had made up my mind that I was going to sea and that was that!

I wrote to a number of shipping companies applying for the position of a deck cadet. I think, in all, I must have written to nearly thirty different companies (hard to believe there were that many when we look at the state of the British merchant fleet today). I was accepted on the waiting list of some companies: the Anglo-Iranian Oil Company (British Tankers), the Blue Funnel Line (Alfred Holt), Reardon Smith's of Cardiff, the Anchor Line, the City Line, Andrew Weir and Crawford's of Glasgow, but was very pleased when I received a letter from the Clan Line, requesting me to attend their office at 109, Hope Street, Glasgow, for an interview. On a warm June morning in 1943 I arrived promptly at ten o'clock at the reception desk in what today would be described as a very old fashioned office. I was extremely nervous and together with the heat in the building I started to perspire.

The receptionist directed me to the marine department. I can remember looking at the lovely models of the company's ships in beautiful glass cases on my way through the corridor to the marine superintendent's office. A rather gruff individual asked me what I wanted; on showing him my letter I was told, "Wait there and I will see when the marine superintendent can see you. He is a very busy man, you know." On my part it was "yes, Sir, no, Sir" as I was sure that he was a very important person. When I think about it now, he was only about thirty and possibly a clerk in the department, but he did have an air of authority about him.

Cadet John Moffat, at Beira in 1946

Ten minutes passed and I was ushered into the office of the marine superintendent. I recall his name was captain MacKinlay; he was very pleasant and made me feel at ease. The interview lasted about twenty minutes, when he had ascertained that my education was to the standard required and that I was in good health, although a medical would be arranged at a future date. At the end of the interview he said, "The company has a waiting list of at least thirty boys and we have lost quite a number of ships, so we may not be able to offer you an appointment for quite a long time. You would be well advised to try elsewhere in the hope that you will get a berth by the time you are sixteen." Earlier in the interview he had mentioned that it was normal practice in the Clan Line to accept boys from Conway, Worcester and Pangbourne and at least some form of pre-sea training was necessary. At the age of fifteen I had little hope of getting into these schools and the three month pre-sea cadet training course at the Royal Technical College in Glasgow was fully booked up for the next twelve months. I had told Captain MacKinlay that I had written to a great number of companies but without success. His final remark was, "Well you could try and get on the 'Pool' and join as a boy seaman."

I replied, "Yes, Sir, I will try and do that." Needless to say I was a bit disappointed and on finding myself standing outside the office in Hope Street, I thought I would go up to the Baron Line in Bothwell Street and try for a vacancy there.

I had been advised by a friend who had spent a lot of time in tramps, "Should you not be successful with Clan Line, try 'Hungry Hughie's', they will normally take cadets with or without pre-sea training. You will find it tough, cadets are just cheap labour, but they will make a seaman out of you." I was prepared to work hard and the thought of being cheap labour did not worry me. (The name Hungry Hughie's does not need any clarification, although I do not think they were quite as bad as people made out.) I went to their office and got as far as the front desk when I was told, "We have hundreds of applicants for a cadetship in this company and we don't need apprentices at this time. Good day to you." I eventually caught the train home to Irvine, feeling a bit downcast. That evening I discussed the position with my parents, neither of whom were very keen on the idea of my going to sea. I was determined, though and in 1944 managed to get a berth as a cabin boy on a small ship, an explosives carrier, having explained to the master that I was keen to serve my time as a seaman and eventually try for a second mate's certificate; at least he gave me a few words of encouragement.

I had written to Clan Line informing them what I was doing and I received a reply wishing me every success and that my name would remain on the waiting list in the event that a vacancy might arise. I assued from the letter that they were going to accept this sea time as part of my training. Work was hard on that ship but the officers and the West Highland seamen taught me a great deal, to ensure that when I did join the Clan Line, I would not be 'as green as grass'. I now had a discharge book, a seaman's identity card and the silver MN lapel badge. I was a Merchant Seaman, although my rating was that of the lowest member of the crew.

I enjoyed my time in that ship, and occasionally got a couple of days at home. I came home on leave on the 7th May 1945 to find a letter had just arrived from the Clan Line. I still remember the wording:

> "Dear Sir, A vacancy for a cadet has arisen on one of our vessels, at present in the Port of Hull to which we would be pleased to appoint you. You will accordingly report to our agents, Messrs William Brown Atkinson & Company Limited Monday the 14th May, who will advise you of her name and location in the port.
>
> Kindly acknowledge receipt of these instructions.
>
> Yours faithfully."

I posted my letter of acceptance the same day.

I was at home when the war finished with Germany. As I only had a week's leave, my time was taken up buying my kit as per the list supplied by Clan Line. On monday, the 14th May, I arrived in Hull, reporting to the agent's office. The agent was a very pleasant man, who advised me that I was to join the *Clan Forbes* berthed in the King George the Fifth dock. The agent organised a taxi for me and I was soon on my way there. The docks were full of ships, all painted grey and I can still remember a few of the names: Brocklebank's *Macharda*, Silver Line's *Silveroak*, a Fort class ship, two Liberty ships and the *Baron Inchcape* (I think that was her name, but I am not certain). I sighted the *Clan Forbes* berthed at the western end of the dock, stern to the quay and secured to a buoy forward. She looked beautiful, as her cargo from India was being discharged into lighters. I got out of the taxi

John Moffat: A Cadet's Adventures

The Clan Forbes in *wartime colours*

The Clan Forbes in *on peace-time duties*

and was prepared to hump my two suitcases up the gangway to the poop-deck. A very jovial docker looked at me, smiled, grabbed one suitcase and helped get my gear up the gangway.

The first thing I noticed was the smell of ghee and curry; the ship was manned by a Lascar crew and of course there were two crew galleys aft. I think that smell had an effect on me, as I was never to become a lover of curries. The Indian quartermaster (Secunny) accompanied me to my cabin which was amidships, abaft No 3 cargo hold. Accommodation for engineer officers and cadets was one deck up from the main deck with outside alleyways running fore and aft, with the cadets' cabin at the forward end. An Indian steward opened a door and informed me that this was my room: quite a large cabin with three bunks, all on the same level, no settee, a table, three chairs, a washbasin with cold running water, three wardrobes and a fan mounted on the after bulkhead (no air conditioning in those days!). The cabin was alongside the engine room bulkhead and even in the UK it was warm. There was a small rug on the wooden deck in the cabin. The two other cadets were on leave but there was a note lying on the table from the senior cadet telling me which bunk was mine. Placing my two suitcases on the deck, I looked at the steward who said, "You follow me, we go see the Burra Malim Sahib." (I later learned that this was Hindustani for Chief Officer.)

Following the steward along the outside alleyway, the deck wood-sheathed and spotless, we descended a ladder on to the main deck (again sheathed with wood) and passing No 3 cargo hold we went up a ladder to the deck officers' quarters. There appeared to be plenty of deck space as all the cabins faced forward. The bridge deck, master's deck and the officers' deck appeared like a small block of flats, a common design for Clan Line ships built around 1937-38.

The steward pointed to the chief officer's office saying,"You go see Burra Malim" and departed, leaving me standing there. As I was about to knock on the door, it opened and out came a very thick-set individual wearing three gold bands on his sleeve. He looked at me and said, "Are you the new cadet?" I saluted and said,"Yes Sir." We shook hands and he asked me if I had found my cabin. We then had a discussion and he was surprised when I said that I had spent a number of months at sea as a cabin boy and that this was my first ship as a cadet. He said, "Well at least you have had some good practical training and you should find your feet quickly on board here." He then told me to go and settle in, unpack and report to his office at 1400.

After unpacking I had lunch in the saloon. The food was very good and there appeared to be plenty of it. I had expected to eat in the messroom and so was surprised to find myself in this lovely dining area being served by an Indian steward. The *Clan Forbes* was a lovely ship and I was very proud to be a memebr of her company. Dressed in a boiler suit I reported to the chief officer at 1400 and given my first job. There was a large cupboard next to his office and I was told to clean it out and then there would be some gear to be stowed on the shelves. Needless to say, the chief officer supervised my work. I found myself without a knife to cut open the cartons of stores and suddenly a voice said,"A sailor without a knife is like a woman without a ****. Here you are, have this one." I thought the chief officer very kind. Unfortunately he was not the sailing chief officer but the relieving one, until the ship's regular chief officer returned from leave.

With the exception of the third officer and chief engineer all the officers were just standing by, until the sailing officers returned from leave. It was regular company practice, that when an officer was appointed to a ship he was usually there for nine to twelve months. When the ship was on a regular run, each officer would take voyage leave. The war had altered this arrangement, though and a number of the company's ships had been absent from the UK for periods of twelve to eighteen months. My first day's work on board ended at 1700 and I was told to go and clean up as dinner was at 1800. After dinner I had a walk ashore but returned early and soon was asleep in my bed. From leaving my home in Irvine at six o'clock the previous evening, I had spent fourteen hours travelling and then a day's work on board. It had been a very exciting twenty four hours, though.

The *Clan Forbes* had arrived in Hull from India with nearly 9,000 tons of much-needed commodities. She was discharging cargo around the clock: castor seed, groundnuts, bonemeal and linseed; six tons of groundnuts had even been stowed under the forecastle head, to maximise the load. The next morning I was called at 0630, washed, shaved and dressed and reported to the chief officer at 0655. I was told to clean my cabin, work with the ship's carpenter for the day and learn the layout of the ship. Chippy was a grand chap; he was aged about 65 and if I remember correctly had been to sea in sail. I should mention that all ships in the Clan Line with Indian crews carried a British carpenter, who had officer status and Chippy and we cadets dined at the second sitting for meals in the saloon.

The Clan Forbes, grossing 7,529 tons, had been built in 1938. She had five cargo holds, No 1 hold being on the forecastle head. It had steel hatch covers and was served by two, small derricks. Cargo could even be stowed on top of the hatch under the forecastle head; the managers of the Clan Line did not waste space! No 2 hold was the largest, stretching from just abaft the forecastle right along to two feet forward of the amidship house. This hold had been constructed especially to carry large steam locomotives to India and South Africa and was served by five deck cranes: a jumbo derrick with a safe working load of 80 tons, two smaller derricks at the forward end with a safe working load of 15 tons and two derricks aft on king posts, about two feet forward of the amidship house and both had a safe working load of 10 tons. The hold consisted of a lower hold, lower tween deck and upper tween deck and the floors were especially strengthened for heavy cargoes.

In No 3 hold, there were two deep tanks in the lower hold, which could also be used for water ballast if needed. The tanks were often used for carrying case beer and had to be secured. This was a big job for Chippy and the cadets as there were about two hundred bolts and nuts for the tank lids. With water ballast every bolt and nut had to be in place and secured. This hold also had an upper and lower tween deck. White lead and tallow was used to seal the grommets. No 4 hold had a lower hold, lower and upper tween decks and had an array of deck cranes, a jumbo 50-ton derrick, two 10-ton and two 5-ton derricks. In the smaller No 5 hold, the lower hold was divided by the shaft tunnel and there was a large security locker in the lower tween deck, mainly used on the outward voyage from the UK for the carriage of bullion or whisky cargoes.

So that was the business end of the ship. Her engines were twin screw triple expansion engines with two Bauer-Wach exhaust turbines working in conjunction with each engine, giving the ship a speed exceeding 15 knots. She also had six double-ended Scotch Boilers and could be steamed on coal or oil. When using oil, the second engineer had 50 day workers in the engine room; when burning coal the number was reduced considerably, as the number of men required on boiler room watch was so much less. The ship's company numbered 130, plus the wartime complement of DEMS gunners, when I joined her. The officer complement consisted of a master, four deck officers, three radio officers, three cadets, a chief engineer and seven engineer officers, a medical officer, purser, assistant purser and the carpenter. There were twenty stewards, three cooks, thirty sailors, serang (bosun), 1st tindal (bosun's mate), 2nd tindal (2nd bosun's mate) and the equivalent number of petty officers in the engine room. Last but not least were two cassabs (one as storeman in the engine room and the other as lamptrimmer on deck). What a far cry from the tiny complement of a ship today!

During that time when I worked in harbour with Chippy, he taught me a great deal and always encouraged me to do what was correct. He was a strict disciplinarian but a man whom I learned to respect and admire. He soon taught me to take soundings of the various tanks, which had to be entered in the sounding book each morning, instructed me in the intricacies of the windlass, chain locker and the mooring winch aft, all useful knowledge to a young cadet.

Discharging was completed and we moved up towards the eastern end of the dock to load for the East. The dockers worked around the clock to complete loading by the 14th June, 1945. The sailing officers had now returned from leave, aswell as the other two cadets. Life changed a lot for me: I found myself a general dogsbody as the other two were much older than I. The chief engineer, Mr Robb, came from the same area as I in Ayrshire and when I got to know him he was a very fatherly figure: someone I could talk to when I felt a little homesick.

We sailed for the East in mid June, in convoy to Dover and then the *Clan Forbes* steamed on along to Gibraltar. I was on watch with the second officer, an excellent man to sail with, strict but fair. In many ways he was my mentor, as he was the officer responsible for cadet training and he certainly gave me every encouragement to keep up with my studies and do the Apprentices Correspondence Course. A call at Gibraltar for orders was followed by a visit to Port Said where we hoped to receive mail from home, but no luck. My first passage through the Suez Canal was very exciting, though. The convoy system was almost non-existant and homeward-bound ships were required to tie up and allow outward-bound ships to pass. One ship that we passed in the Canal was the *Empress of Australia*, loaded with military personnel returning home after a long spell overseas. That night, little did I think that, four years later, I would sail in that fine ship as Fifth and eventually as Fourth Officer. Twelve hours later we arrived in Suez and anchored in the bay to take on oil and water. On the 27th June we were on our way to Aden; in the Red Sea, it was hot, to say the least and soon I was suffering from the inevitable prickly heat.

All three cadets were now on daywork and our job was cleaning out the lifeboats and refilling the water tanks. I was beginning to acquire a tan but had been well advised not to expose my skin too much to the hot sun. The senior apprentice (he was an apprentice and not a cadet) had advised me to buy a topee at Port said; it certainly protected my head and neck. From there we made a call at Aden for orders and then on to Bombay. The southwest monsoon was blowing quite strongly, we experienced a lot of rain and the sea was rough but the *Clan Forbes* was a good sea ship and we hardly noticed the movement. On the passage to Bombay we were employed chipping the deck under the forecastle head and applying red lead to preserve the steel work. The usual practice on a Clan Line ship, was chip and scrape outward and paint on the homeward run.

The Indian crew had overhauled all the cargo gear on the outward passage and as we approached Bombay, we were all ready to discharge cargo. The night of the 9th July was spent unloading deck cargo before sailing and on the 16th July we arrived at the Sandheads to embark the Hooghly Pilot for the passage to Calcutta. The pilot boarded, immaculately dressed in white uniform and pith helmet, followed by his entourage, a helmsman, leadsman, steward and, if I remember correctly, his own cook. He only spoke to the captain. He epitomised the British Sahib and truly represented the British Raj. Calcutta is about 170 miles inland and as we made our passage up river it became hotter and hotter. We changed pilots at Budge Budge (the oil terminal) and then there was another change of pilot before we started the passage through the dock system. The senior apprentice had mentioned that on a previous trip to Calcutta he had counted something like sixty engine room movements in an hour. On this occasion I counted something in the region of sixty five.

We had two steam tugs, belching out filthy, black smoke which almost choked the bridge team. Slowly moving through the vast dock, we passed Britsh India Line ships (two names, I recall, were *Howrah* and *Tanfield*, both apparently loading coal), City cargo liners and the *Clan MacInnes*, a very old Clan ship built in the early 1920's. American built Fort and Liberty ships were discharging and loading cargo on each side of the dock and just astern of our berth was the *Macharda*. During my time in Hull I had made friends with her four apprentices and we had had some good runs ashore; now I was able to renew our friendship.

After all the port formalities were completed and we had been passed by the Indian doctor, discharging commenced. For the next three weeks the winches hardly ever stopped, except for repairs. The entire Indian labour force wore khaki uniforms and were known as the Defence Force of India Docks. Coolie labourers were privates, winchmen had lance corporal stripes, cranemen were corporals, hatch foremen were sergeants and the ship's foreman was a sergeant major. I can always remember this fellow, an Anglo-Indian called Sergeant Major Pope: when he spoke to a ship's officer his voice was very soft but when he had occasion to reprimand a member of his workforce, if he was down Number 5 Hold aft you could hear him quite clearly on the forecastle head. Anglo Indian officers, lieutenants and captains would visit the ship at odd times throughout the day and night; they were known to us as the 'office wallahs' although most were very pleasant people. Work for the cadets consisted of looking after cargo lamp clusters, rigging arc lamps and generally inspecting cargo running gear to ensure that it was all in good working order. Another job was to paint the draught marks; we used our little jolly boat for this, being very careful to ensure that no paint was spilled on the gunwales of the boat.

Our Indian crew paid off and went home on leave and a stand-by working party looked after derrick gear and ships maintenance. Both deck and engineer officers worked very hard. Boiler cleaning and other engine room repairs were being carried out and engineers were often required to do 'field days', eight hours watchkeeping plus two or three hours working at the winches on deck at sea, and ten hours per day in port.

The summer of 1945 in Calcutta was the hottest and most humid on record. It was almost impossible to sleep in our bunks at night but if we decided to sleep on deck it was not a wise move as we were usually bitten by mosquitos or washed off the deck by heavy rain. I rather envied the cadets on the Brocklebank ship: they slept ashore in the Marine Club, lovely cabins with huge fans on the deckhead. Clan Line sadly did not follow the example set by Brocklebanks and B.I.

I did go ashore in Calcutta, to visit the shopping centre, 'chowringhee' and visit Firpo's, famous for its food and wine, but as a poor cadet I could not afford to have a meal there. Anyway, I doubt if I would have been allowed in as only the 'Raj' appeared to be welcome. Calcutta was not a good port, there appeared to be an invisible barrier confining merchant seamen to an area of the city where they could be both exploited and unacknowledged. Europeans and Anglo-Indians whom I encountered almost looked on me as an untouchable. (I re-visited Calcutta after independance and those of the British Raj who had remained, together with the Anglo-Indians, were very pleased to accept an invitation from a second officer to come onboard for a drink and supper.)

The arrival of our mail at Calcutta was marvellous and we got all the news from home. Our own letters for posting had to be given to the third officer and one of his many duties was to censor mail before it was given to the agent for posting. This of course was common practice in the war years, for obvious reasons.

Our outward cargo had consisted of large amounts of military stores and equipment, including beer and spirits and all logistic supplies for the 14th Army which was still fighting the Japanese in East Asia. When discharging was completed, the cadets worked with Chippy, repairing cargo battens in the holds, limber boards, cleaning bilges, testing strum boxes and sweeping the holds. Wood was easily obtained in Calcutta and so it was the practice to renew wooden battens where necessary. Lots of mats and dunnage wood came on board as the next cargo to be loaded was jute, tea, pig iron, castor seed and a further consignment of tea at Colombo.

Our Indian crew rejoined about six days before we sailed; there were a few new faces, but all the petty offficers were the same as before. In those days the Indian crew usually all came from the same area and quite often the serangs brought the men from their own villages, giving excellent continuity as far as the chief officer was concerned. We sailed from Calcutta and rumours around the ship were that we were possibly bound for Europe but there was no specific mention of a UK port. One bright spark thought that we might receive orders to sail south for South America or even New York. The master, Captain Andrews, said that we would receive our final orders after we had completed loading in Colombo.

Sailing from Calcutta we had an uneventful passage down the Hooghly. Our work consisted of re-storing the lifeboats. To ensure that their stores, consisting of tins of Pemican, chocolate, biscuits, barley sugar and condensed milk were not stolen, we had de-stored the boats during the river passage to Calcutta. The chief officer was most particular about preventing theft from the lifeboats and indeed from any other part of the ship. In ports such as Colombo, Aden, Suez and Port Said, a security watch was maintained at all times, which was, without doubt, a very wise precaution.

In blacked out conditions, cabins hot and stuffy, we had the swell and wind fine on the starboard bow, the southwest monsoon blowing strongly. Three days after leaving Calcutta we arrived at Colombo where we secured to buoys and commenced loading cases of tea and topped up with fresh water. We were not allowed leave ashore, except for the senior apprentice, who was given special permission to visit a close relative. Twenty four hours later we sailed from Colombo with orders to proceed to Le Havre and Boulogne to discharge all cargo save 1500 tons of tea, for which we would be told the port of discharge later.

Our fourth officer had been promoted to third officer and transferred to the *Clan MacGillvary* in Colombo and the senior apprentice was now permanently on watch with the chief officer. As we steamed towards Aden on a northwesterly course, doing a good fifteen knots, the weather improved each day. On the third night out from Colombo we were informed by the master that Japan had surrendered after atom bombs were dropped on Hiroshima and Nagasaki and now the war was over. As the ship was at sea we only had a mild celebration that evening, but next day there was work to be done with large axes to break down all the wooden blackout partitions and strip down the black canvas curtains; a job that everybody enjoyed immensely!

Three days later we arrived in Aden; we had six hours to fuel and sailed in the afternoon on our way to Suez. The passage up the Red Sea was hot but this time we could have our portholes open day and night and so we had a certain amount of air circulating around the accommodation. Four days later we anchored in Suez Bay. After loading fresh water and provisions, we proceeded through the Canal to Port Said. A few hours in Port Said, discharging some military cargo we had loaded at Aden, and we were on our way towards Gibraltar. There had been one other Clan ship in Port Said, I think it was the *Samfield*, on her way home after a voyage lasting two years. Six days later we passed Gibraltar and after rather a rough passage, with wind and ultimately fog, we passed Ushant on our way to Le Havre, where we entered harbour twelve hours later.

The port was a shambles and our fine ship came into contact with a number of submerged objects, luckily without any damage to hull or bottom. As soon as we were secured in the harbour, barges came alongside with lots of dockers aboard and soon the hatches were open and we were discharging. We were allowed leave ashore in Le Havre. Other apprentices whom we met at the Seamen's Club were very helpful and were able to advise us on what we should do and where to find the night life! The people in

Le Havre had suffered badly in the war, and everyone we met was terribly anxious to buy chocolate and cigarettes.

A week later we were in Boulogne and again when entering harbour we were lucky not to damage the ship. The people were starving, it was a piteous sight to watch the dockers cluster around the midship galley and the two after galleys. On completion of discharge at Boulogne we received orders to proceed to Glasgow to complete discharge and go into drydock. We anchored at the 'Tail of the Bank' where we would then make our way up river to Merklands Wharf on Sunday. I was then to have my first leave home!

There was a number of Clan Line ships in Glasgow, still painted in their wartime grey colours, but their funnels were painted in the company house colours of black with two red bands (often referred to as the Blood of the BI, who were our keen trading rivals). After two weeks leave, I returned to the *Clan Forbes* as she was loading for India, to call at Calcutta and Vizagapatnam. Like the other Clan ships, we still had our wartime grey paint, but our funnel was painted in the Clan Line colours.

We loaded general cargo for Calcutta, including, again, beer and spirits for the army and various sorts of military cargo. At Calcutta we would load jute and tea to bring to the UK. The cargo for Vizagapatnam mainly consisted of all the material needed to build a ship: steel plates, pipes, engines, boilers and all, as the local shipyard there was to build the first twin screw ship for the Scindia Navigation Company. Our heavy derricks were to be used to discharge this cargo into specially constructed barges in Vizagapatam Harbour. We would then load iron ingots, ore, linseed and oil cake.

Christmas Day was spent at anchor waiting for the Hooghly pilot. We eventually berthed at Kiddapore Docks two days later. The weather in Calcutta was more clement than it had been on my first visit, but I got a bout of malaria and had a very uncomfortable three days sweating it out. Luckily we had a good medical officer on board who was a specialist in tropical diseases. We finally completed loading on the 8th January and we sailed, bound for Liverpool and Glasgow.

This was the ship's thirteenth voyage; on the thirteenth day of the voyage a man died. It was a strange thing indeed, but became stranger still because, as our crew were Moslems, only the captain was asked to attend the burial service. Still, work went on. With the senior apprentice on watch with the chief officer, the other cadet and I spent a great deal of the voyage chipping grey paint off the bridge house and red leading where necessary. We were also employed sewing new canvas screens to be attached to the rails on the monkey island. After the canvas had been soaked repeatedly in water and stretched as tight as a drum, it had to be painted white. Most of the voyage to Gibraltar was spent painting the ship in her peacetime colours.

Unfortunately, before we sailed through the Straits of Gibraltar, we had an oil spill, when the engineers, while pumping up the settling tanks, caused an overflow. The wooden boat deck was awash with black fuel and so was the wooden deck around No 3 cargo hold. The chief officer and chief engineer were both very upset, however an all-out effort was made to clean up the mess and this was accomplished in record time. By the time that we arrived at Point Lynas to pick up the Liverpool pilot, the ship was immaculate. It was now mid-February 1946 and the weather in England was very cold. We were not the first Clan Line ship to arrive home in full peace time colours, this honour had gone to the *Clan Cameron*, when she docked in Christmas 1945, in the Victoria Dock in London.

On arrival at Liverpool, we found the docks very congested, but what a lovely sight to see, ships in peace time comlours, all the well-known British companies, Harrisons (Two of Fat and One of Lean) Cunard passenger and cargo ships, Canadian Pacific, New Zealand Shipping Company, Federal Steam Navigation, one of Tatems, a Smiths of Cardiff tramp, the *Bradford City* and the *Olivebank*, owned by Andrew Weir, and, built in about 1926, I think she was the oldest ship. On my last visit to Liverpool in 1984 it was very sad to see the docks so empty, and to think that it is very doubtful if one will ever again see such a representation of the British Merchant Navy, as I had seen that day in 1946. I often ask, where did we go wrong?

Still, to continue, we eventually berthed in the Canada Dock and commenced discharging. The company's marine superintendent in Liverpool came aboard and congratulated the master and chief officer on the appearance of the ship. The same congratulations went to the chief and second engineers as the engine and boiler rooms were immaculate together with all the deck machinery. And it all worked!

Part of the cargo was discharged at Liverpool and then it was up to the Princes Dock in Glasgow for final discharge, and then the ship had to be fumigated, for on the last two voyages, cockroaches had been very much in evidence, although we did not appear to have any rats on board. Then we would start loading, with one of the first peace-time cargoes for South Africa after the end of the war. A fortnight later, when I returned from leave, she was loading machinery, including locomotives and heavy cases, aswell as whisky in the security locker in No 5 lower tween deck. Loading was completed by the 27th February and the Liverpool pilot boarded (he boarded in Glasgow to ensure that we did not waste valuable time picking up the pilot on the way into Liverpool). We then sailed for Birkenhead and locked in at Clan Line's regular berth in the Vittoria Dock on the following afternoon, to commence loading in the evening.

The *Clan Murdoch* and *Clan MacNair* were also at the loading berth, the former loading for Bombay and the Malabar coast, the latter for Calcutta and other ports on the east coast of India. On the opposite side of the dock there were three Blue Funnel ships loading and a Bibby liner at the West Float. I also remember that the old Anchor liner *Castalia* was preparing to sail for India from the East Float berth. Docks on both sides of the Mersey were full of ships and there were also regular sailings of troopships and passenger vessels from the Landing Stage. I remember seeing the great White Star Line's *Britannic*, the Cunarders *Samaria*, *Scythia* and *Ascania*, Canadian Pacific's *Duchess Of Bedford* and a New Zealand Shipping Company vessel. I always enjoyed visiting Liverpool, there was good entertainment at Atlantic House; the Apostleship of the Sea, the Flying Angel, Missions to Seamen and the Gordon Smith Institute for Seamen all had dances at least once or twice a week. The real advantage, of course, was that they were cheap: we cadets were not well paid, so a visit to the Mish was a priority!

Loading of the holds at Birkenhead was completed on the 8th March and after the hatches were battened down, eight, specially constructed horse boxes had to be loaded, each containing a racehorse bound for South Africa. They were very valuable animals and every precaution had to be taken on the voyage to ensure that they arrived safely at Cape Town. The senior apprentice was told by the chief officer that it would be the cadets' job to look after the horses and clean out the boxes every day; how charming. A large number of bags of bran were loaded together with bales of straw and hay. A humane killer was also given to the chief officer, in order to comply with regulations for the carriage of livestock; fortunately the horses travelled well and the gun was not required. That day we sailed, bound for Cape Town, Port Elizabeth, Durban and Beira in Portuguese East Africa and the port for Rhodesia.

The pilot disembarked at Point Lynas and we soon worked up to a full 15 knots. We cadets turned to each morning at 6 o'clock to feed and water the horses and try to clean out as many boxes as possible before breakfast at 8.30. We had awful weather out to Cape Finisterre, though, with gales and rough seas and the poor horses looked very sorry for themselves. A beam was fitted in each box, to try to stop the horses from being too uncomfortable in its temporary stable, but the horses were very seasick; they were not vomiting, but were just looking sad and swaying back and forth on their legs. Apart from a comforting pat on the back and talking to them, there was nothing more we could for them, though.

Three days after sailing, the weather started to improve and although we were rolling in the long Atlantic swell, it was a gentle movement. Each day now the weather improved and soon we were just working in shorts and sandals (but wore white or khaki uniforms in the saloon for meals, of course). Looking after the horses was almost a full time job: most of the morning was taken up feeding and watering them, then we cleaned out the boxes and covered the floor with fresh straw. We groomed the horses regularly, but this was not a pleasant job in the tropics as both beasts and cadets sweated heavily.

General deck work for the cadets consisted of overhauling cargo running gear, renewing wire runners, repairs to guys, rope splicing and lots of other work. We usually were employed all afternoon on this work, with a ten minute break for tea. Food on the *Clan Forbes* was excellent, we hard-working youngsters had good appetites and wasted nothing. At 4.30 pm it was time to start the evening feeding and watering sessions for the horses again. They tended to become very thirsty and we seemed to be carrying endless buckets of water from the deck fresh water pump to the boxes. Another watering followed at 8 o'clock, and then the horses were battened down for the night. The boxes were well-ventilated so the horses had a good circulation of fresh air and were made most comfortable at all times. After a shower I just fell into bed and was asleep within minutes.

With a six hour bunkering stop in the Cape Verde Islands we pressed on for Cape Town. During our nineteen day voyage we had a heavy work routine and there was little time for study. We were not given any time off for study, for the chief officer insisted that we studied in our own time, not his! He was a fair man but a bit of a task-master. He was also approaching the time when he would be promoted to master, as it was common knowledge in the Company that the managers considered him to be an excellent officer.

On the 25th March we sighted Table Bay. It was truly a magnificent view, there was not a cloud in the sky and the mountain with the Devil's Peak and the Lion's Head made a beautiful sight. The senior apprentice remarked, "We are now arriving in the Land of Milk and Honey." How true his words were.

With the pilot embarked, tugs secured fore and aft, we moved slowly towards a berth in the inner harbour, five or ten minutes' walk from the city. Soon we were secured and the usual port officials boarded. After the ship was cleared and the 'Q' flag (for 'quarantine') hauled down, the agent came on board and soon we were reading our mail from home. Mail is top priority when sailors are away from home and most agents ensure that it is delivered as soon as the ship is berthed.

The horses were to be off-loaded as soon as possible and their owner's agent was soon onboard inspecting each animal. Thank

Heavens he seemed pleased with what he saw. As he disappeared with the chief officer to discuss discharge arrangements, the second mate said to us, "Maybe you three will get a few bob from the trainer as he appears well pleased with the livestock; keep your fingers crossed."

The boxes were soon on the quayside and we went ashore to take each horse out of its shipboard home. They were a bit shaky to start with but soon found their shore legs. We had great difficulty with one, she was not keen to leave her box, but with some sugar lumps and lots of straw on the dockside we got her out. I think that we were sorry to see them leave: although it had been hard work looking after such valuable cargo, we had become rather fond of the horses. The second mate's remark about the few bob actually came true. The senior apprentice was called to the chief officer's office at about 4.00 pm and came back to our cabin with £15, five pounds each. Well, as my monthly salary was only £12 10 shillings five pounds was a large sum to receive and I really felt rich. Watches were almost unobtainable at home, so I bought a good watch in Cape Town.

In that part of the world the people like to come into the dock area to look at the ships. Unlike the British Raj in Calcutta, the people in the Cape were (and as far as I know, still are) very hospitable to British seamen. Great entertainment was organised at the Flying Angel Seamen's Mission with a dance every evening. The chief officer had decided that two cadets should be on day cargo duty and one on night, but as the shore labour only worked until 8.00 pm, all three of us had plenty of time off. We had five days in Cape Town, it was really super, we made lots of friends and the 'Mission Girls' were terrific. Chocolate and ice cream sundaes galore – and silk stockings! They were in great demand in the UK, so it was wise to buy a few pairs for my girl friend back home.

We were nearing completion of discharge at Cape Town and a big job for officers and cadets was to ensure that all cargo had been discharged for that particular port, as the chief officer was not amused if we over-carried anything to the next port. The ship also always had to be searched for stowaways before we sailed. The five days passed all too quickly and soon it was time to sail for Port Elizabeth, about 36 hours steaming from Cape Town. We encountered the Cape Rollers rounding the Cape of Good Hope and experienced heavy weather most of the way to our next port. On the passage to Port Elizabeth we were gainfully employed overhauling our accommodation ladder, re-varnishing the woodwork, renewing the ropes used for lowering and raising the ladder and we managed to get a real shine on the brass treads. The forward 80 ton jumbo crane was also rigged and tested, as we had locomotive parts to discharge at our next port of call.

The approach into the bay again was very picturesque, not as impressive as Cape Town, but it looked as if it might be a good run ashore. We docked in Port Elizabeth on a Sunday afternoon, the 31st March, and there were crowds of people on the dock to see us berth. What a welcome, we thought; as there was a Union-Castle passenger liner docking there, however, we soon realised that almost the entire community had come down to the docks to see her; it was an added bonus to the crowd to see us tie up. The authorities cleared the ship very quickly but the agent told us that no dock labour would be available until 7.00 am next morning. We went ashore, but being Sunday, of course, everywhere was closed.

Five days were spent in Port Elizabeth and again we were most grateful to the people who extended so much hospitality. Even though food on board was excellent, at about 10.00 pm we always felt hungry and would stop at a small cafe on our way back to the ship and enjoy the luxuries forgotten by a war-rationed UK of a large plateful of steak, eggs and chips, costing half a crown (25 pence). I bought a lot of foodstuffs in Port Elizabeth to take home, dried fruits, tinned meat, tinned fruit and tinned jam, all strictly rationed at home.

We sailed from Port Elizabeth on Friday the 5th April and arrived at Durban the following day. Durban has a very fine harbour and the approach is just as picturesque as the other ports on the Coast. With pilot embarked and tugs secured, we proceeded to a bunkering berth on the famous Durban Bluff. We spent the entire day loading fuel oil, to ensure that we had enough bunkers to last until we reached Aden or Suez. As we made our way towards our berth, we saw quite a few ships loading cargoes of coal. One Greek ship in particular I recall, she was about 5,000 tons and looked as if the accommodation had been stuck on as an after-thought: it looked just like two shacks on deck, with a woodbine funnel. She was loaded almost to her marks and looked very dirty!

There was a Baron Line ship, a Union Castle wartime-built Empire ship painted in Union-Castle housecolours and two British tramps. We completed bunkering that evening and then washed down the decks before moving to our discharging berth in Point Docks, not too far away from the main gate. We had a lot of cargo for Durban and so were to have about a week here. We were well out of the water by now, and the chief officer decided that work on the boot-topping would commence and two cadets would paint the draught marks while one cadet would be on cargo watch.

There were many fine ships in Durban Harbour flying the house-flags of distinguished British companies, like British India, Andrew Weir's Bank Line, Bullard King & Company, Harrison Line and Union-Castle. Durban was a good run ashore and I remember meeting good friends there, having a sightseeing tour and beach parties, and not forgetting a trip to the Valley of a Thousand Hills. Once again there was a very good Flying Angel Mission in Durban. I believe that the padre, a man named Precious, had served in the Clan Line before taking Holy Orders. He and our second mate were great friends, I think they had been apprentices together, before the war.

We sailed on the 14th April, bound for Beira, and our senior apprentice remarked, "Well, the good time is over, no more civilised ports until we get home." This did not cheer us; still, Beira was our final port of discharge and first port of loading. We arrived at Fairway Buoy three days later, embarked our pilot and proceeded to an anchorage, to await an available berth. There were many ships at anchor, most of them flying the Red Ensign. Two very old Clan Line ships were alongside loading, the *Clan MacIlwaith* and *Clan Matheson*. We spent three days at anchor and when the *Clan Matheson* sailed, loaded right down to her marks, we moved alongside to occupy the berth she had vacated.

We completed discharge of all outward cargo on the 25th april, holds were swept clean and bilges and strum boxes inspected, cleaned where necessary, tested and the limber boards replaced before loading commenced. We were to commence loading large copper ingots and tobacco, then to proceed to Tanga and Mombasa for further loading. Round the clock working was the practice in Beira, where the big job for us was painting the hull and getting the draught and plimsoll marks almost to artistic standard. The chief officer was most particular about this, he was a perfectionist and expected us all to be likewise.

Since arrival in Cape Town we had become used to the noise of steam engines moving wagon loads of cargo day and night, belching out black smoke. The practice was the same in Beira, where the engines seemed to be older and made a great deal more noise. All the locomotives burned coal and there was black soot everywhere, although it was quite surprising how clean the wharves were, where native labourers were continually sweeping and washing the area down. Our gangway always looked clean, as the secunnies washed it down two or three times a day.

We all had bouts of fever in Beira, the worst affected was the senior apprentice. Despite the best of attention from our medical officer, he was only partially fit when we sailed for Tanga on the 1st May. Once we got to sea, though, every body felt better. We had a four day passage to Tanga, arriving there on the 4th May. Four days were spent loading hemp and sisal, then on to Mombasa, which we reached on the 9th. This was to be our final port of loading on the African Coast. On proceeding alongside, we noticed that the ship berthed ahead of us was an old British cruiser, HMS *Jamaica*, in port for rest and recreation. We loaded drums of oil and fat, bags of coffee beans and soda ash. During our stay in Mombasa all overside painting was completed and our hull looked superb.

We sailed on the 12th May, loaded to our marks, bound for Marseilles and London. The passage to Suez was a pleasant one, lots of superstructure painting and scrubbing wood decks. The funnel and masts had been painted in Tanga and the derricks still had to be painted, but as soon as we entered the Gulf of Aden, the chief officer decided that the weather was ideal for doing the stays a mixture of white lead and tallow. We had good weather all the way to Suez, and luckily no sandstorms in the Red Sea. On arrival at Suez we bunkered, topped up with fresh water and collected our mail. We spent the 23rd May transitting the Suez Canal and at 11.00 pm we passed the Fairway Buoy at the entrance to Port Said and were on our way to Marseilles.

Taking advantage of the weather, the painting continued at a rapid rate, as we wanted most of the outside work completed before arrival at Marseilles. On the 26th-27th May we steamed through the straits of Messina and past the volcano Stomboli; it was not too angry as we only saw puffs of smoke coming out of the crater at regular intervals. On the 28th we arrived at the Fairway Buoy, to await the pilot. We steamed around for about an hour and eventually an American naval patrol boat signalled us to stop and remain where we were. The patrol boat slowed down and when he was twenty feet off our starboard bow, a voice on the loud hailer roared, "Follow me Cap and I will pilot you through the dredged channel." We were later informed that the channel had only recently been swept and declared free of mines. The harbour was in ruins, but I do recall seeing the famous Chateau d'If and at the time I thought it looked very sinister.

A pilot boarded us inside the breakwater and eventually we tied up alongside a berth which appeared to be one of the few that had not been reduced to rubble. We spent about twelve days discharging cargo, working night and day and a lot of the wool that had been loaded in Beira was discharged into barges. We were allowed shore leave in Marseilles; it could be termed a sailor's paradise, and a good time was had by one and all.

On the 8th June we sailed for the London River, berthing in Tilbury in the afternoon of the 14th June. I was about to have some home leave now and was due for a change of ship, but I had no idea where I would be sent. Before leaving the ship, we were told by the chief officer that white topped caps were to be worn. This was peacetime practice from the 1st May to the 1st September but had been discontinued during the 1939-45 War, and the practice was reinstated after the Victory parade in London in 1946. Some time in the late 'fifties or early 'sixties it was decided that white-topped caps were to be worn all the year round.

The *Clan Forbes* continued in service until 1959, when she was broken up at Hong Kong. Perhaps I should just conclude my story of her with the observation that, when wartime experiences are recounted, the *Clan Forbes* always seems to come into the picture.

After a spell of leave at home, I was appointed to the *Empire Might* and joined her in the Canada Drydock in Liverpool on the 18th July. The ship was under the Ministry of War Transport and managed by Blue Star Line at the time and on the 18th, which was handover day, there were Blue Star officers, Clan Line officers and other representatives of both shipping companies. Various documents were signed and the *Empire Might* came under Clan Line management, when her name was changed to *Clan Macrae*. She was still painted in her wartime grey, and looked really scruffy compared to the *Clan Forbes*, which surprised me as the other Blue Star Line ships in the port looked so smart. I think her previous cargo must have consisted of apples, as we cadets spent a lot of time cleaning rotten apples out of the bilges. We had a lot of work to do.

As John Moffat sailed for Swansea on the 25th July, he was no longer a green young man hankering for the sea but confident of the course for his profession and passed each examination to reach the exalted position of master. He would leave Clan Line for Canadian Pacific, where he gained much experience in large liners, but reached the pinnacle of his career as a highly respected master with the Royal Fleet Auxiliary. In his own words:

An RFA Master has far more opportunity to handle his ship than his opposite number in the commercial world. Shiphandling experience is gained during 'Helicopter Operations and Replenishment at Sea', when two or more ships are being replenished with fuel, stores and ammunition. This operation is accomplished with ships steaming at twelve knots, distance apart 120-160 feet for a period of three to five hours. It is often necessary for course to be altered 20 to 180 degrees, this evolution is carried out in steps of ten degrees at a time, ensuring that after each completed step, all ships are steaming on the same heading, maintaining speed and distance apart, before the next turn is ordered. During heavy weather and in blacked out conditions, this operation can be a little hazardous, as there is very little room for error.

"Very little room for error": that phrase, so apt to the profession of Master Mariner, must surely apply most of all to the world's pilots – and the greatest of them all was Jack Holt.

---

* Grateful thanks are extended to the publishers of 'Sea Breezes' who previously published some of the material contained in this Chapter under the authorship of Captain Moffat.

JACK HOLT – THE PILOT OF THE SUPERLINERS

Jack Holt's grandfather, Robert Pearce, was a pilot, a highly professional job with the responsibility for the safe docking and sailing of shipping, passengers and cargoes. These were the grand Victorian days when British trade and commerce undoubtedly ruled the waves, and the merchant marine was the pride of the Empire. Among the chief of the country's ports from the earliest days of steam navigation, was Southampton. This is how *The Channel Pilot* described Southampton so many years ago:

> "The volume of trade at Southampton is enormous. The chief imports are live stock, grain, hides, wool, cotton, coffee, coal, tea, tobacco, fruits, and provisions; the exports, general merchandise. Besides numbers of large sailing ships and steamers privately owned, at least 18 steamship companies, with fleets in the aggregate greatly exceeding half a million tons, use this port in times of peace."

The pilots' greatest skills were demanded by the owners of the greyhounds of the seas, the express passenger mailships of P and O to India and the Far East, Royal Mail to South America, Union-Castle to South Africa and the companies that raced across the Atlantic, headed by the White Star Line. Millions of pounds worth of 'high-tech' tonnage, countless millions of pounds worth of passengers and their valuables, all needed the highest care and protection; it was the job of the pilot to assure that protection, navigating the busy lanes into and out of port and nursing the ships through docking operations in all sorts of conditions. The pilot had to be a skilled Master Mariner and was one of the most respected men in the professions of the sea. It was a deadly serious job, as Ruth sang in 'The Pirates Of Penzance':

Extract from Jack Holt's indentures. The wording had hardly changed for generations, and would hardly change for generations to come.

> "When Frederick was a little lad he proved so brave and daring,
> His father thought he'd 'prentice him to some career seafaring.
> I was, alas, his nursery maid, and so it fell to my lot
> To take and find the promising boy apprentice to a pilot."

Three of Captain Pearce's sons joined the pilotage service of Trinity House. One son, though, chose the career of Master Tailor. His son, Jack, was born at 82 Above Bar, Southampton, over his father's shop, on the 22nd February 1902. The sea captured Jack's imagination, though and he had no wish to be a tailor – but a pilot. So did his two cousins. The pilotage service was simply in the family blood.

When Jack left King Edward's School in 1916 he was to join the Imber Line as a cadet. Sea time and certificates would eventually lead to qualification as pilot. The Imber Line was a company famed for the beauty of its windjammers, vessels that were the last word in sailing ship technology. So Jack was first to be indentured under sail. The company had two ships, one in distant waters, the other due home shortly, when Jack would join her. Sadly, though, she was sighted by a German submarine in the English Channel and torpedoed. The Imber Line had no other ship in which Jack could sail, so he joined instead a London-based company, Harris and Dixon, a steamship company tramping around the world. He signed his indentures on the 16th May 1916. The conditions of his service are fascinating to read today:

> "....John Robert Pearce Holt hereby voluntarily binds himself Apprentice unto the said Harris and Dixon Ltd, his Executors, Administrators, and Assigns, for the term of four years from the date hereof; And the said Apprentice hereby covenants that, during such time, the said Apprentice will faithfully serve his Master, his Executors, Administrators, and Assigns, and obey their lawful commands, and keep his and their secrets, and will, when required, give to him and them true accounts of his or their goods and money which may be committed to the charge, or come into the hands, of the said Apprentice; and that the said Apprentice will not, during the said term, do any damage to his said Master, his Executors, Administrators, or Assigns, nor will he consent to any such damage being done by others, but will, if possible, prevent the same, and give warning thereof; and will not embezzle or waste the goods of the Master, his Executors, Administrators, or Assigns, nor give or lend the same to others without his or their licence; nor absent himself from his or their service without leave; nor frequent Taverns or Alehouses, unless

upon his or their business; nor play at unlawful games: IN CONSIDERATION WHEREOF, the said Master hereby covenants with the said Apprentice, that during the said term he, the said Master, his Executors, Administrators, and Assigns, will and shall use all proper means to teach the said Apprentice or cause him to be taught the business of a Seaman, the sum of twenty pounds deposited with Messrs Harris and Dixon Ltd to be returned intact on the satisfactory completion of four years apprenticeship,.."

All this, for the princely sum of £60 for the four years: in the first year, he would earn ten shillings a month, in the second year twenty shillings, the third year thirty shillings and in his fourth year he would earn forty shillings a month.

Jack was to join the *Heliopolis*, a coal burning ship grossing 4,928 tons, built in 1905 as a tramp, to steam around the world for the cargoes that made the best profit they could find. In 1913 she had been purchased by the Admiralty for conversion to a hospital ship but on the 7th March 1916 she was sold to Harris and Dixon. Now, at the end of May, he would join her at Glasgow, where she was sailing for Boywood, Newfoundland, to bring back a cargo of paper for the 'Daily Mail'.

Conditions on board were spartan. With no refrigerator on board, milk and butter were best used up quickly and all the meat was salted; the crew chewed on the same sort of beef that their predecessors had done for centuries. After three or four days the fresh vegetables ran out and they had to make do with dried peas and potatoes. In the forecastle the crew were from Hong Kong and inevitably there was a language barrier. Jack learned just two Chinese phrases:

1. A nameless swear word.

2. "What time is it?"

She would run across the North Atlantic, unaccompanied, avoiding enemy torpedoes as best she could. On one occasion, homeward-bound, they were to rendezvous with six ships off the west coast of Ireland, forming a convoy, which was a system developed during the war whereby ships sailed together in an effort to limit the enormous losses being caused by enemy submarine attacks.

During the night, four of the ships had been sunk by an enemy submarine and in the first light of day they saw the stern of the fifth ship going down. Then they spotted the submarine: it was coming to attack them. The refuge of Dingurban Bay was a long way off and the only way they could make it would be to try to outrun the submarine to find safe haven.

Every man on board who was not needed on watch had to work in the stoke-hold that day. As they made all steam the ship raced for refuge but the submarine gave chase furiously. It was the hardest, toughest day in Jack's young life – and they just managed to outrun that German submarine.

In May 1917 the Canadian Pacific Line acquired the ship, crew and all, and she was renamed the *Methven*. She now served the war effort with cargoes of cotton, turpentine and iron ingots. Jack spent half his time learning seafaring skills in this twelve year old ship carrying difficult cargoes and the other half straining every nerve to detect and avoid enemy attack. In fact he received a commendation by a Master for his very efficient signalling, a crucial job in Atlantic convoys, where communication could be very difficult, but vital to every ship.

Jack's apprenticeship was not without romance. The ship was running to Savannah in the United States. When they went ashore, Jack and two friends would attend the Presbyterian service in the local church, where the minister declared how the congregation was showed up in its devotion by these three English boys here, the like of whose singing he had never heard before! The traffic manager in Savannah was the son of a Lancashire immigrant who had hopes that his daughters would marry good English boys, and urged Jack and his fellow-cadets to take his daughters out to an ice-cream parlour. One of the girls grew especially fond of him and her father asked him to leave the company and he promised to find a job for him there. Jack was keen to pursue his career at sea, though and in any event would not desert his country, still in the grip of war.

Having survived the war, one could not imagine that any other harm could befall one – certainly Jack did not when he went to a tea dance in Vancouver. All that he can remember is waking up in a Vancouver hospital: he had caught the 'flu in an epidemic which killed almost as many people as the war had. Jack was lucky to recover.

When he finished his apprenticeship in 1920, Canadian Pacific's marine superintendent in Vancouver pressed Jack to stay with C.P. and go to the school of navigation there. Jack had his heart set on the pilotage service in Southampton, though, and decided to return there, sailing back to Liverpool on the *Montrose*. He graduated from navigation school and at the age of seventeen Jack joined BP Tankers as Second Mate. He served a lot of time in the Persian Gulf in the *British Soldier*. One day, he saw a Goanese chief steward called The Butler come on deck with a newspaper and spread out the newspaper on the top of the bunkering hatches midships. Jack wondered what he was doing and asked The Butler, who replied:

> "Sahib, this is what you call oatmeal. In hot weather all the weavils come out of the oatmeal into the sunshine. Then I can pick them out."

Jack hurriedly told Apprentice Tucker to throw the whole lot over the side but The Butler was scandalised; suspecting that Jack had taken leave of his senses, he insisted that Jack sign an entry in the log.

In April 1922 Jack obtained his Mate's Certificate and qualified as Master in 1924: he was just 22 years old. It is quite possible that he set a record as the youngest master under the British flag. To prepare for the pilotage service, Jack joined the James Towing and Dredging Company in January 1931, so that he could gain local knowledge of Southampton Water and the port area. The mundane workhorse that was Jack's first command was the *Stonewell*, a dredger towing barges in and out of the port as they dredged Number 7 Dry Dock.

On the 23rd June 1931 Jack obtained his Pilot's Licence and started service on the Isle of Wight Inward Pilot Service. On the sailing cutter *Totland* Jack would spend a week on board and then one ashore, although when the traffic was heavy, he would frequently be called back. For his first three years Jack served as a second class pilot, taking only vessels that had a maximum draught of 17 feet, such as timbermen, small coastal tankers and colliers: home traders, bound for Northam and Eling Wharves. They were not obliged to have a pilot, although it was preferable. He still had time to fall in love, and in 1933 married Phyllis, whose father was an engineer in the Royal Mail Line, running to South America.

At the beginning of 1935 Jack was appointed as a first class pilot, when he brought in the *Ile de France*. This 43,153 ton Atlantic greyhound owned by the premier French company CGT had been built in 1927 and was said to be the most beautiful ship afloat. For several years she carried more first class passengers than any other ship on the North Atlantic. Within a few months, though, Jack's most awesome task yet awaited him when he was instructed to bring in the French Line's *Normandie* on her maiden voyage. It was the 29th May 1935 when the liner proceeded up Southampton Water. Grossing 79,280 tons, her turbo-electric engines drove four screws to make record crossings of the Atlantic. She was truly the last word in style, the very embodiment of French culture that for so long has been the envy of the world, and she would later constantly vie with Cunard's *Queen Mary* for the Blue Riband. Jack would travel over with her from her call in le Havre in order to avoid wasting time and fuel by stopping to pick up a pilot en route. So Jack was able to sample the inimitable style of French living and the world's finest cuisine in the course of his career!

The French Line was delighted with Jack; apart from anything else, they only usually got old men as their pilots! He was an excellent pilot and regularly brought in the French Line ships, not only the *Ile* and the *Normandie*, but also the *Paris, de Grasse, Cuba, Antilles,* and *Flandre*.

For Jack's service to the CGT, the French awarded him the *Chevalier de l'Ordre du Mérite Maritime* on the 26th April 1956. This raised a sensitive diplomatic problem, though: when one of Queen Elizabeth I's noblemen was awarded a French decoration, she was so outraged that she had him beheaded. The British never forgot this – they would not dare – and after Jack was given his decoration he received a letter from the British hierarchy warning him that he could only wear the medal in France, or in the French Consulate or in French ships, but never on British soil.

French ships formed only part of Jack's story, though. As the U-boat menace subsided in 1944, the Government decided that it was safe to bring into Southampton the great superliners from Cunard's fleet, now trooping and carrying whole battalions at a sailing, the *Queen Mary*, *Queen Elizabeth* and *Aquitania*. Jack's job now was to bring in the Queens, as a prelude to what the following years of peace would hold. War was still raging for Southampton when on the 19th April 1945 he was piloting the United States ship *Examiner*, a very fast cargo ship, from St Helens Roads to Cowes. The captain suffered an injury, though, and was rushed to Ryde Hospital with a broken collar bone that had damaged his lung. The chief officer only had a mate's ticket and a message was received by morse, on the authority of the United States Navy, Trinity House (the UK pilotage authority, Jack's employer) and the United States War Shipping Association, instructing Jack to assume the position of Master, and proceed to take the ship to the Bristol Channel. Perhaps a unique experience?

The Inward Pilotage Service was a dangerous job in the war; it was the only service that worked outside the boom defences where ships were degaussed against magnetic mines and really there was nothing to stop the Germans capturing them, which of course would have caused chaos for all the shipping that depended on the skills of the pilots. Jack joined the Outward Pilotage Service in 1945, when peace would follow shortly – and, of course, all the peace-time travel which that meant.

Soon, though, this meant that he had to face a dilemma: he was asked to stay as the chosen pilot for the Cunard liners, but as their sailings clashed with the French Line departures, he could not pilot the French liners aswell. He therefore had to choose between the two, and so he chose the Queens, although he would still serve the French Line when he was not needed for the Cunarders.

So, Jack became the Number One Pilot for Cunard, nursing the mighty *Queen Mary* and *Queen Elizabeth* throughout what was to become the most distinguished sailing partnership in maritime history. Perhaps it was the *Queen Mary* that just had the edge in the nation's affections; from the time of her launch on the 26th September 1934 she captured the hearts of the people. The post-war years were the busiest ever on the North Atlantic. Between June and September the Queens were often filled to capacity. They were the fastest ships on the run, of course, and indeed the *Queen Elizabeth* was the faster of the two, although because of the enormous cost of running them both at full speed, it was the 'Mary' who was given her head, and so she held the Blue Riband for year after year.

In June 1952, the American *United States* crossed the Atlantic on her maiden voyage averaging 35.5 knots, breaking the 'Mary's' best record of 31.6 knots, set in 1938. As the *United States* overtook, her master gallantly signalled to the 'Mary' that he was sorry for taking the Blue Riband from her, to which, it is said, the master of the *Queen Mary* replied in the true traditions of the British merchant service:

> "Not at all, Old Boy; anyway, a real lady does not like to be seen in fast company."

The 'Mary' remained the pride of Southampton and the Merchant Navy, and over the years she had become so much a part of Southampton that Sotonians would take her magnificent sight for granted, just as they do the Bargate or the spire of St Michael's Church. On the 31st October 1967 she sailed from the port for the last time. The weather was awful but Sotonians turned out in their thousands, patiently waiting to say goodbye to an old friend, as a Royal marines band on the dockside continuously played 'Auld Lang Syne'. She was as beautiful as ever, with a huge paying-off pennant and thousands of brightly coloured streamers linking her still to the quayside. As she inched away from the Ocean Terminal, she must have felt touched as everybody said their own farewells, an amazingly personal event, for they knew that, whatever happened in this world, there would never be another *Queen Mary*.

By this time, British deep sea shipping had already shrunk enormously. Air travel had taken away so much passenger shipping trade that huge tonnages were lying idle because there was no work for them. To make matters worse, the overheads involved in employing UK crews were growing so high that whatever profits were being made, were getting swallowed up by costs. It was becoming prohibitive to maintain the ageing fleets of transatlantic liners and the economic climate gave no incentive to build new, more cost-effective ships.

Because of all this, the pilotage work for Jack became a shadow of its former self. By the time that he was elected Captain of Southampton Master Mariners' Club for 1971, the glittering 'Atlantic Ferry', the creme of the world's fleet, had quietly disappeared. Just the *Queen Elizabeth 2* would remain to keep the service alive; highly appropriate, indeed, that it was Jack who piloted her out of Southampton on her maiden voyage.

Looking back on his career piloting the world's greatest luxury liners, Jack's view was that all the big ships handled much the same. The really awkward one was the French Line's *Liberté*, with her arrangement of forward and after engines that made manoeuvring her into berth difficult. For all their size, the Queens were beautiful to handle. Jack surrendered his Pilot's Licence when he retired on the 11th June 1969, completing very nearly 38 years' service during which he became one of the most distinguished pilots in the Trinity House service.

At the Club's annual shipping festival service in June 1989, the colours of Jack's old service, the Trinity House Isle of Wight Pilotage service, were finally laid up in Winchester Cathedral. Now the pilotage authority was to be Associated British Ports, who own Southampton Docks and the port area, and the ancient institution carried out by Trinity House, served by Captain Jack Holt and his family, was brought to an end.

NORMAN LUCAS – SCENES FROM BRITISH INDIA

The Indian sub-continent lies across the main lines of communication between the industrial Western Hemisphere and the rich but underdeveloped East. The British, French, Dutch, Portuguese, even the Danes sought in turn to establish themselves as ruler of that vastly important peninsula. The potential of trading there was enormous for the shipping community after the East India Company lost its trading monopoly in 1853 and there was promise of very big returns indeed.

A certain Robert Mackensie was a Scots merchant in Ghazipur who had established his business in the 1830's. He was acquainted with a fellow native of Argyleshire named William MacKinnon who arrived in India in 1847 to take up employment at a sugar mill near Calcutta. In December of the same year they entered into partnership. The firm prospered as general merchants but soon they realised that they would profit by carrying their own goods in their own vessels aswell as offering deadweight capacity to carry other people's goods, thus profiting in all ways from operating their own ships.

In 1854 the East India Company invited tenders for a mail contract between Calcutta and Rangoon, which promised a guaranteed, regular income, the most persuasive of all incentives for the growth of shipping. The firm was determined to win the contract with a service fully operated by steamships and in September 1856 they registered the Calcutta and Burmah Steam Navigation Company Limited. Soon the company was operating two 500 gross ton, iron-hulled, screw-driven steamers, the first steamships to sail from Britain to India in a twelve-week voyage.

As the company flourished it was restyled the British India Steam Navigation Company Limited in 1863, when many of their routes were still only badly charted and were very hazardous, which in fact led the early B.I. masters to perform their own surveys as they went along. The result was outstanding efficiency and the company prospered, well ahead of any competition who hesitated to operate in uncharted waters.

B.I. was given huge assistance when they secured a whole series of mail contracts and trooping agreements and their performance was so impressive that a virtual partnership between B.I. and the government developed over the years. By the difficult years of the turn of the century the company almost single-handedly made a shipping centre of Rangoon, which became an important link in the long chain of communication between India, the Far East and Australia. All sorts of cargoes were carried to Rangoon, from where the company started also a service to Australia which continued for many years. B.I.'s work spread westwards, too, to Africa, which was quite a watershed in the business' dvelopment and Sir William MacKinnon was responsible for so much of the development of East Africa that in Mombasa's Treasury Gardens, a statue was erected to him after his death in June 1893.

After he died, MacKinnon's leadership was assumed by James Lyle MacKay, later to be a great name in British merchant shipping as Lord Inchcape. He, too, was a Scot. His secret of success?

"I never fail to keep my word and I always clear up my desk at night."

An outstanding businessman, MacKay had to face the emergent nationalism of the Indian peoples aswell as their infant fleet. He also had to combat the heavily subsidised fleets of Germany and Japan, aswell as other British and European competition on B.I.'s routes, which all made for such a cut-throat situation that in 1902 the Colombo Conference was formed, regulating market factors of freight rates and passages. It was an uneasy truce, but the company's principles remained as dependable as possible in such financially troublesome times.

In 1906, the year in which Norman Lucas was born, the company had a fleet of 116 ships, all specially designed and built to serve the sort of runs that B.I. operated. This was the company that Norman was to serve for all his working life from dogsbody cadet to Master of all he surveyed. This is his story.

How did I, coming from a non-seafaring company, come to be mixed up with the sea and with B.I. in particular?

As far as the sea was concerned, the answer is fairly simple. From our house in Lawn Road, Southampton, we overlooked the docks and could see the masts and funnels of the great liners. I found that I liked travel and it was also a good way to get away from home. And why B.I.? Again, a simple answer: my parents knew a B.I. captain. By this time, the company had merged with another mighty name in the business of shipping. For many years B.I. had worked closely with the Peninsular and Oriental Steam Navigation Company, in a useful relationship in which B.I. ships could serve Indian and Burmese ports not covered by P and O. It came as no surprise that the two companies eventually merged, in 1914, and although on paper it looked like P and O had absorbed British India, the former's chairman, Sir Thomas Sutherland, retired and was succeeded by B.I.'s Lord Inchcape. Moreover, for many years P and O's agents in India would be the respected firm of MacKinnon Mackensie and Company, managing agents of British India. The merged organisations now seized a pre-eminence in shipping that has never been lost; the combined fleet of 187 ships of a million and a quarter deadweight tons was larger than most navies.

There was I, then, a month after my sixteenth birthday, in a brand new uniform walking up the gangway of *Woodarra* in the Royal Albert Dock, London, not knowing what to expect in this new life but intent on enjoying it. The *Woodarra* was one of six of a class bought from the Government at the end of the First World War. She was laid down as the *War Apollo* in 1919; her gross tonnage was 7,946 tons with a length of 465 feet and a speed of $12\,1/2$ knots, quite a good speed for those days. She had five holds and two between decks throughout and was built to carry refrigerated cargo. Her cadets were housed in No 3 between deck in two watches. There were about half a dozen of us new this trip but we soon settled in; about half of us worked on deck with the other half at school! And a few getting bridge experience. As usual we went out to Australia around the Cape of Good Hope and back via Suez.

In order to avoid calling at Cape Town for bunkers we carried a between deckful of coal which we transferred to the bunkers shortly after rounding the Cape. I found muscles which I didn't know I had! It was good fun, though. Shortly after leaving home we new boys had to perform a concert well enough to escape a ducking in cold water. I was glad that I had learned to play the piano! We also had the usual Crossing the Line ceremony. On a future occasion I was to be Neptune's wife. On this first voyage we were to see one of the last commercial sailing ships, *Mount Stewart*, on passage between Cape Town and Australia. We circled her and took photographs for we knew that all too soon, such a sight would be a mere memory on the world's seas.

On the way from Cape Town to Australia we regularly saw the biggest of swells, for there was nothing to stop them all the way around the world there. On our arrival at Melbourne there were one or two sailing ships at anchor; I didn't take much notice of them at the time, which of course I regret now, looking back.

Australia is a huge country. It takes nearly a month for a 12 knot ship to go right around it. The longest is the eastern side with weather conditions in Tasmania similar to ours in England, right up to the North. Melbourne and Sydney have similar weather to ours but not quite so freezing. By Brisbane at the bottom end of Queensland tropical weather starts and one gets the real feel of Australia. Most large places are much alike all over the world and it is not until one gets into the country towns that the unique feel of Australia comes over one.

In one of the Queensland ports we cadets were entertained by a farmer who, it turned out, owned a pineapple plantation, and he invited us to help ourselves. It was the best pineapple that I have ever eaten. Commercial pineapples and fruit in general are picked before they are ripe and lose that last bit of sun that sweetens them. Another port that we visited in Queensland was Port Alma, the port for Rockingham several miles inland. There was only a jetty with a shed for the wharfies to live in, a shop and a post office and beyond there were mudflats for us to play football on. Unfortunately several billion sandflies lived there too and fed off of us; their bites last a long time.

The Australians were kindness itself to us cadets, many of whom, particularly in Queensland, had come out on B.I. ships. We used to spend quite a long time in port discharging and loading, a very different thing to the matter of hours that container ships have today. True, their leave conditions are better but I am sure that the quality of life is not. All of our voyages on the *Woodarra* were to Australia except one, when we went on a Houlder Brothers charter to South America, in fact to Buenos Aires to load a frozen cargo for home. One thing sticks out in my mind on that voyage: we were about to leave Santos in Brazil when the Liverpool firemen refused to work. The Old Man settled that by ordering the engineers to fire her to get outside the 3-mile limit when refusal to work became mutiny, a very different thing. There was no trouble after that.

On one voyage home from Australia we sailed via the Cape. When off Angola we had a fire in the bunkers which were in No 3 lower hold. It then spread to No 2 hold but we eventually put it out after taking some of the cargo out to get at the seat of the fire and poured CO_2 down the hatch, so starving the fire of oxygen. I am glad to say that the company was appreciative of our efforts.

The time came for me to sit for my first examination to become an officer. This duly obtained, I reported to the company and was appointed 4th officer of the *Mashobra* for the voyage to Calcutta, when I would be transferred to the company's service in their eastern empire which extended from the Persian Gulf to Japan, controlled from Calcutta. *Mashobra* and her class were really cargo ships with some passenger accommodation carrying about 200 first and second class passengers. They were a little over 8,000 tons with a maximum speed of $12\frac{1}{2}$ knots. They ran from London to Bombay, London to Calcutta and London to East Africa, sailing on regular dates, and they were very popular, if you were not in too much of a hurry. Having said that, no two ships in the company were ever identical, although there were fifteen ships built in *Mashobra's* class by a variety of companies who each had pet ideas. In one case that I know of, it was only the differing heights of the wireless aerials that distinguished them.

Being a fourth officer is only a little different from being a cadet but at least you have a gold band instead of buttons on the cuffs of your jacket to give you a bit more status. You were not allowed to keep watch by yourself and only east of Aden to take the daylight hours of the chief officer's watch, which I soon discovered was just as well. Confidence gradually rose with experience, though and in Calcutta I was promoted and appointed third officer to the *Gogra*. One of the jobs of the fourth officer was to look after the passengers' baggage; when it came on board the wanted-on-voyage baggage had to be separated from the not-wanted-on-voyage baggage. Of course, somebody had packed the baby's bottle in the not-wanted-on-board baggage. Fortunately I was able to oblige and received an invitation to "Come and see us in Blackpool".

So now we come to Calcutta, that wondrous place 120 miles from the sea. Well, I had heard of this river, of course, and looked it up on a map which as usual failed to tell me anything of what it was really like. The first thing that we saw was the pilot cutter which spends one month on station while a sister ship was in Calcutta. River Hooghly pilots in those days were one of the gods of Calcutta society. The pilot came over in a boat with his servant and a mountain of baggage, while not far away was a lightship marking the outer shoals. The water by now was very muddy so that even if there had been no lightship we should have known we were in shallow water. After a couple of hours passing more lightvessels, a lighthouse appeared. This was Saugor Lighthouse on an island. The land right up to and past Calcutta is very flat and the mouth of the river is very wide. By and by, clumps of trees appear, aswell as signs of habitation. Gradually the river narrows and one can see both banks. Because of areas of shallow water, ships always go up the river on a rising tide and the tide current gets up to at least 5 knots.

Very soon comes the most awkward part of the navigation upstream: at a place called Hooghly Point the river takes a smart righthand turn, with only a narrow channel to go through. As the bow of the ship passes the point it loses the force of the flood tide and the tide on the after section of the vessel carries on pushing the stern half so that the forward half wants to head for the bank. It is a matter of timing the rudder movement right to forestall this. A great sigh of relief when this is safely negotiated! There is a smaller one like this to negotiate further on, though.

Fortunately the mud is very soft and vessels can be got off if they run aground, but it is not recommended: bad for the captain's heart. By now there is more traffic on the river; fishing vessels all over the place and floating haystacks on their way to Calcutta. Signs that we were approaching a city appeared and soon we were in Garden Reach exchanging pilots. If berthed in the river, alongside a jetty or not, chains had to be used owing to the strong tides and therefore another four hours work had to be put in. It was all very interesting the first time but a chore after 35 years of it!

Thus my introduction to India. I did not have long to think about it as I joined *Gogra* in Kidderpore Docks. At the far end of Kidderpore Docks there were half a dozen or so berths for loading coal which was a very valuable export from Calcutta. It was mined in Bengal and Bihar and sent to Rangoon, Madras, Mandapam, Colombo and other places for ships bunkers, steam trains and gas works. I must have carried well over a hundred thousand tons in my time. Coal is not such a bad cargo to carry as you might think as it is easy to wash off, unlike cement. Another thing is that you cannot damage coal, so no nasty letters have to be answered, like, "Please explain why...." or, "We fail to understand why...."

The coal that *Gogra* was carrying, unusually, was to be discharged at Marmagoa, the port for the Portuguese enclave of Goa on the west coast of India. After this we were to proceed to Bombay to load cotton for Shanghai, a very promising start to my Indian coastal service. The *Gogra* was one of sixteen sisterships bought by the late Lord Inchcape at the end of the First World War, grossing 5,181 tons with a maximum speed of 10 knots. These ships were of the three island type with one between deck, two hatches forward and two aft with one between the bridge and the engine room. They carried mainly coal, rice and timber, the last two to all ports on the east and west coasts of India.

The trip to Shanghai was very interesting and we lay astern of HMS *Hermes*. Shanghai was a very bustling place, the waterway was full of all sorts of ships: ocean liners, passenger ships, coasters and junks from up the rivers. We returned to Calcutta and then had various runs until I was transferred to the *Angora*. She was a ship of 4,289 tons built in 1911 by William Denny and was a fine looking ship. She was on the Rangoon mail run and could do a good 16 knots, a speed of greased lightning after the 10 knotters. There were three ships on the run and they connected with the English mail to and from Calcutta. It was a very prestigious run, and of course had been the company's first. The English mail left Calcutta at about 9.00 am every Sunday with the senior partner to see us off and we had 49 $1/4$ hours to get from Port Limits to Port Limits, or be fined. It was a highly regimented effort.

I was destined not to last long on this run as while the ship was under survey in Calcutta I was rushed to hospital with what turned out to be dysentry; I must say, I did feel poorly overnight. Once on the mend, though, I enjoyed myself and made friendships which have lasted to this day. After I recovered it was decided that I needed further recuperation on a ship running out on the troopings and to my great joy was appointed to *Santhia* for a passage to Australia. What could be better! It was a run which we all tried to get as Australia was as near to Heaven as we could expect to get while on the coast.

Santhia was one of three sisters built by Swan Hunter in 1925, grossing 7,753 tons with a speed of 12½ knots. She carried a few first and second class passengers and a large number of deck passengers who bought a straw mattress on board which they spread on deck. There were special cooks from whom they bought their food on the voyage. This was the system on all the passenger mail runs. We were soon clear up the Hooghly and on our way to Freemantle via Java to pick up some bananas. We were also going to Adelaide, Melbourne, Sydney and Newcastle New South Wales where we were to bunker and prepare to pick up horses for the army in India.

On our arrival in Adelaide we found that the stevedores were on strike and in some crafty way we managed to stay alongside the wharf the whole time while other ships anchored outside to avoid port dues. A whole month in Adelaide! We made many friends, mostly among the female population; memories still linger on. After discharging our cargo of gunnies for the Australian wheat, horse stalls were built on deck and in our two between decks. Fodder was loaded in the holds and Australian grooms looked after the horses on the voyage to Bombay via the Torres Straights. In Bombay I was promoted to Second Officer and stayed with the ship, with responsibility for her navigation, which I greatly enjoyed! As far as I was concerned, to stow the cargo safely and deliver it in good order at the right port was what going to sea was all about. I am afraid that I did not like the housework part of the job which, because of the war, lasted for 15 years.

Our next voyage was from Calcutta to Japan via Singapore and other ports. There was a very happy relationship all around the ship and we used to go ashore in Japan together and had a lot of fun. On one voyage after leaving Japan I found that I could not get warm, I developed a fever and, worse, spots. Yes, I had smallpox, courtesy of Shanghai. I was left behind in the isolation hospital in Hong Kong with what turned out to be only a mild case, as I had been vaccinated when I was a child. As a European in the hospital I was spoilt by the nurses, but eventually the last spot dried up and I was fit enough to mix with the outside world again. I was in a hotel for a week waiting for a ship to take me back to Calcutta and fortunately my favourite nurse was having a week off so I had a good guide to show me around the 'island'.

Hong Kong is full of hills and there is a marvellous view of the harbour after a ride on the Peak Railway where you look down to see flotillas of small boats and larger ones moving in the harbour. For comparison looking down on Cowes from 2,000 feet in Cowes Week would help. Whatever the size, all the junks have one thing in common: Mum, Dad, the children, granny, dogs, pigs, hens, all live on board together.

My recuperation complete, back in Calcutta I found myself appointed second officer on the *Hatkhola*. She and two other ships, the *Hatarana* and *Hatipara* were built in Japan in 1917 for the British Government and bought by B.I. Collectively known as the 'Topi' class, they were general purpose ships liable to be sent anywhere. After a fairly short time I found myself back on the Calcutta – Rangoon mail run as Extra Second Officer on the *Aronda*. After only one voyage the second officer suddenly died and I took over from him. The reasons for frequent changes were many: death, promotion, sickness and leave.

By now I was getting used to which ship was on which run, steaming between Calcutta and Rangoon on the mail run aswell as sailing from Calcutta to the Far East, via Rangoon, Penang, Singapore and Hong Kong. From Rangoon there was a mail run to Madras, a service to Vizagapatnam, a weekly run to Chittagong and one to Tavoy and Mergui, to the south of Rangoon. Another service ran from Madras to Penang and Singapore. Different ships served different routes, being designed especially to suit the nature of each run, and all the steamers carried not only cargo and first and second class passengers but also Indian deck passengers, as cheap labour was much in demand in Rangoon growing rice and doing other manual work, and in Malaya for the rubber plantations. They went with only the rags they stood in and returned after a period with plenty of this world's goods.

Rangoon was a very busy port: I once saw 22 of my company's ships in port there at one time, all busily loading and unloading cargo, mostly imports of coal and gunnies, and exports of rice and teak. Most of the ships were moored to buoys in the river owing to the strong tides. Rangoon was, I think, a favourite port with most of us. There was a good Mission to Seamen which I used a lot, aswell as a Seamen's Club. There were also cinemas and places in which to eat. A lot of the ports that we visited in India were anchorage ports, far from civilisation with nothing to go ashore for, even if one could. We therefore were able to save a bit in the bank and let off steam when we were in civilised ports.

By the way, the only way to get ashore at Rangoon was by sampan, operated very skilfully by Chittagonians. How many seafarers got back to the ship safely after a skinful is mainly owing to their skill!

By now the time was approaching when my home leave was due; for the last six months, every day was struck off a calendar. I was appointed Fourth Officer of *Mantola* for the voyage home. I arrived home on the 9th September with the prospect of a nice winter leave of seven months to thicken my blood. Thicken my blood or not, four months later I found myself engaged and three months later on my way back to India as a passenger on the *Merkara*.

By now Lord Craigmyle was chairman of the company. Arriving back in Calcutta, I was appointed to Cranfield, one of a class of five ships built in 1919 for the Government and bought by B.I. straight from the stocks. She was ideal for collier work but a bit more difficult to load a mixed cargo for several ports. I enjoyed this sort of thing, I expect it's because I like jigsaw puzzles! We carried coal anywhere between Rangoon and the west coast of India; if to Rangoon always to load rice back. Colombo and Madras were enclosed sea harbours and provided an opportunity to try and sail a lifeboat. It was hard work but good fun. Moulmein was one of the timber-loading ports we went to, just across the Gulf of Martaban from Rangoon. Ships berth at timber mills just outside the small town and it was interesting to watch the elephants move and stack the logs; they were very clever but staunch trade unionists who knew to the minute when it was time to knock off. As there were no taxis it was the agreed thing to get to Moulmein by stopping the first bus, turn everybody off and treat it as a taxi. Nobody was bothered, as time seemed to matter very little. There were only two hotels in town and belonged to an ex-B.I. Goanese steward. It was nice to get away from the main cities.

I was later transferred to *Querimba* going to Australia and back, arriving in Calcutta in November. She was one of three ships built by William Gray in 1925 and grossing 7,769 tons with a shelter deck, she was a big carrier. We loaded the usual gunnies outward and took coal from Newcastle NSW for Singapore. Singapore is a fascinating place, much dominated by the Chinese. We had a run from Singapore to Bangkok in consort with *Khola* and *Kistna*, ships of 1,500 tons. Arriving back in Calcutta, I was taken off to await the arrival of my future wife. She came out to Bombay with a friend on P & O's *Ranchi* and I met her in the station at Calcutta. The great day arrived and we were married in the Carey Baptist Church in Calcutta by a friend and spent our honeymoon up country at Monghyr with another friend shortly before the earthquake of 1934. Their house was destroyed and if it had been a few weeks earlier we might have been too.

November is the beginning of the very short, so-called wet-weather season and is delightful after the hot and sticky late spring and the hot and humid sou' westerly monsoon season with its rain and hot weather that follows when the rain stops. After the honeymoon, I was given the job of looking after *Angora* laid up in a dock in Calcutta. Very suddenly she was put into commission on the Calcutta – Rangoon mail run for a few voyages, but then was laid up in the river at Rangoon. My wife came to Rangoon and shortly afterwards I was appointed Second Officer of *Chilka* running to Cocobada. We got three days in Rangoon every fortnight, which was not too bad.

After three months it was time for home leave. We were sent to Calcutta to join *Dumana* commanded by a gentleman known as South Pole Hudson. As we were passengers, this counted as part of my leave, and was quite a pleasant way to spend it. Homeward bound we called at Plymouth to land some passengers, where we left the ship ourselves and celebrated by going to the theatre and seeing 'The Belle Of New York'. Back in India, the only live theatre we ever saw was done by the Calcutta Amateur Dramatic Company at Christmas time. Again it was another cold leave, but I suppose it was good for me.

The time came for me to return to India but a happy event was expected soon, in July, and a fortnight before my daughter's arrival, the company gave me the job of being officer in charge of *Nerbudda* laid up in the Fal above King Harry Ferry, off Combe

Creek. There was no crew on board and my only companion was an engineer who kept an eye on the engine room. I went to Truro by train and was met by a friend who was looking after another laid-up ship (remember this was the time of the Great Depression, when work was scarce for men and ships). It was the 1st July when I joined, the beginning of another hot summer. On the 15th July I had a telegram to say that I had a daughter.

The next weekend I took a little French leave to have a look at her. After about six weeks when all was well they came and lived on board the ship. I had a small rowing boat and once a week I went to the nearest village to catch the daily bus to Truro for my stores and other shopping, and once a month the agents sent up a launch to take us to Falmouth to draw our pay and collect our lighting and cooking oil. There was plenty of coal and so for the winter I bought a bogy and kept it in the saloon. It was a marvellous set-up. One nasty day in February they sold the ship under my feet to the South American Saint Line. But fancy getting paid for a holiday like that!

Well, we returned home and awaited orders. When they came, I was surprised to find myself promoted to Chief Officer of *Modasa*, one of our homeline ships. The surprise was that I did not think that my name had reached anywhere near the top of the list as promotion was by seniority in our company. To Middlesborough, therefore, I went, not a favourite port of anybody's, nor was the captain helpful, when I could have done with it. Fortunately, when we returned to London I was transferred to *Mashobra*, where the situation was just the opposite. So there I was Chief Officer of the ship on which I had been Fourth Officer, nine years earlier. I spent a very happy 15 months on her. This captain and another with whom I sailed later had a great influence on my approach to command.

After very happy service on this ship, at my request I transferred to the Indian coastal services again. It was decided that my wife and daughter who was by now 2½ years old, should come out to India, so all three of us went out as passengers on the *Mashobra*. Sir William Currie was now our chairman, and a very fine example of a gentleman he was too. Lady Luck looked after me in Calcutta as I was appointed to *Chyebassa* which was on a monthly run from Calcutta to Bombay: a week at each port and a week at sea in between. The only snag was that we did have a lot of moving around in the docks in Calcutta. *Chyebassa* was of 6,249 tons, built in 1907, and felt like it. All the other five of her class had long since departed. After eleven months, a new ship arrived to take her run and I was appointed to my old ship *Cranfield*, commanded by the man who had been chief officer on the *Santhia* when I had smallpox.

So there I was, back on the coal, rice and timber, not knowing where we were loading for next. My wife stayed in Calcutta as we got back there from time to time to load coal. Most of our discharge ports were anchorage ones off the coast in the south of India, and in the northwest off Kathewar up fast-flowing, featureless, muddy rivers. After some time my wife managed to get a holiday on a government farm at Kalimpong and I took local leave to join her. It was good to have a break. To get to Kalimpong from Calcutta, one has to go by train to Silguri and change there at the bottom of the hills to a narrow gauge railway which goes up to Darjeeling. It was a delightful experience.

Returning from this interlude, I reported to the marine superintendent, who in theory appointed us to a ship. He said to his clerk, "What have you for Mr Lucas?", to which he replied, "*Homefield*". At this I jibbed as I would have liked something on a regular run. So the clerk had to try again and this time he came up with the *Erinpura*. This time I hit the jackpot.

Erinpura ran between Rangoon and Madras once a fortnight and we had four days in port at Rangoon. On the 11th July 1939 I joined her in Rangoon with visions of a happy time ahead. Arrangements were made for my wife and daughter to go to Rangoon, but Adolf Hitler upset my plans two months later and very soon we were sent around to Bombay to prepare for trooping for Suez. In a very short time the ship had to be painted grey, between decks got ready for troops and the ship stored.

Four months later we were back in India on the Madras – Singapore run taking the place of *Rajula* which would go on permanent troop carrying as she could carry many more. My wife and daughter went to live in Singapore, though, so it turned out to be a good run. (They were certainly getting around!) We were well out of the way of the war at the time. After four months, we went to Calcutta for survey and there I was transferred to *Warina*, a standard design of ship grossing 3,120 tons built in 1919. Shipping was now at sixes and sevens. All passenger ships were requisitioned aswell as a number of cargo ships and they were used as they became available. On *Warina*, we did voyages to Rangoon, traded around the Indian coast and did several voyages to the Persian Gulf, which was not a suitable place for a ship like this in the heat of summer. We survived, though, and were away from the war zone.

By this time my wife and daughter were back in India and went to live in Darjeeling as it looked like I would be away from Calcutta for a long time. My home leave was now long overdue but home leave at that time looked particularly unattractive, anyway, and when at last I was told that I could take leave in South Africa or in Australia, I swiftly chose Australia, as far south as possible. Tasmania was our destination then, and Hobart in particular, and at last we were parked in the spare cabin of *Ismaila* on our way to Melbourne. I was really ready for leave and began to dread a hitch right up to the time that we dropped our Hooghly Pilot. All went well and after a pleasant voyage we arrived at Melbourne and crossed over to Tasmania by ferry boat, landing at Launceston where we took the train to Hobart. I bought a newspaper and looked for a place to stay, found one, liked it and it suited us very well. So we settled down to a little domestic life. It was the month of November, but summer was just settling in. It was a delightful spot, never getting too hot as even on the hottest day a sea breeze came along in the afternoon.

After five months, the company decided that it could not do without me and I was recalled to join the *Takliwa*, then a troopship, in Melbourne as extra chief officer for a voyage to Bombay. After we arrived at Bombay I was transferred to a ship called the *Cap St Jaques*, a Free French ship which the company was running for the Government, on a triangular service between Basra, Suez and Bombay. She had a French captain and most of the engineers,some of the deck and saloon crew were French, but we had a British chief steward. We really had a marvellous year. The captain left the running of the ship to me and we fed like fighting cocks. Both nationalities got on very well together and, fortunately for me, I had a good working knowledge of French so I was able to brush it up.

Once it came in very handy: we were carrying Polish refugees, men, women and children who had walked a long way to Persia. We were to take them to Karachi where they would be taken to Kenya. The young woman in charge of them could not speak English or French but we found an old lady who spoke Polish and French, so without much difficulty we got her to understand what had to be done when the refugees came on board. They were a pathetic sight to see, but after twenty four hours on board they soon cheered up and then it was a treat to hear them sing.

On one occasion we arrived at Suez to be given the news that we were to stay there several days. The third officer and I received permission to go to Cairo for a couple of days. The ship knew the address of the hotel where we were going to stay so that they could get in touch with us if necessary. We had a marvellous couple of days going to the pyramids and we returned to our hotel late at night unaware that a message was waiting, instructing us to return to the ship sooner than possible. Hurry as we could, we arrived at Suez to find no *Cap St Jaques*.

We went to the sea transport officer, expecting to be shot at dawn. Luck was on our side, however and we were sent to join her at Aden on another transport *Mendoza* which was subsequently lost. We were welcomed back on board with no reproach. I dread to think what might have happened if it had been a real B.I. captain!

After a year of this happy state of affairs, the French managed to find a French chief officer and in Suez I was transferred to *Sofala*. She was a smallish ship of 1,031 tons, engaged in carrying petrol along the North African coast for the 8th Army from Alexandria, a nice port as a base. At that time petrol was carried in flimsies, protected by wooden battens. They used to leak badly and how we did not blow up, I do not know. After a time it was carried in jerricans and 40 gallon drums, which did not leak. Our first call was to Tripoli in Libya, from where the Germans had just been pushed out. This seemed to be the pattern that followed: wherever I went, the war petered out.

Benghazi was an interesting place: the water was so clear that there did not seem enough water to float us. The harbour seemed to be strewn with objects. We became very friendly with the sergeants' mess there, so were able to get our meagre beer ration increased a little. Haifa was another good place, and the Third engineer and I managed to get a couple of days leave to visit Jerusalem. Recently I have been back and it is all so different; the Israelis have done a lot of work between Tel Aviv and Jerusalem and I did not recognise the once-barren hills.

We went to Famagusta in Cyprus and to Beirut a couple of times, and we also went down the Red Sea, once to a tiny port called Yenbo in Arabia to take supplies to the locust control centre. We had to have great faith in the local Arab pilot! We also went to Massawa, the hottest place in the world, to tow a small ship to Suez. In this way, two years passed and the war in Europe was coming to an end, and we were sent back to Calcutta where I was transferred to the *Ellenga*, which after a short while was laid up in Calcutta for survey.

One evening I received an order to join *Pachumba*, leaving next day for the UK, where I would then have leave. Our first stop was to be Massawa where we were to load scrap. This was all very well, but I had just heard that, the Japanese war having ended, my wife and daughter were on their way to Calcutta. I did not have time to do anything about it. It was so hot in Massawa that our captain managed to arrange for most of the officers to have a short stay in the hills above Massawa, staying in the officers mess, and while we were there I managed to get a look at the Abyssinian border.

At last we set sail for Suez and great was my surprise when the agent boarded and greeted me by saying, "We have your wife and daughter in the launch." The ship that we were on, carrying war supplies, was diverted from Calcutta to the UK and on to the United States. Unfortunately, my wife and daughter were not allowed to travel back on my ship and they followed a month later on *Maloja* bringing back refugees from Hong Kong. I was allowed to stand by my ship in Liverpool until they came home so my leave did not start until then.

Ten months later, when I had nearly forgotten what going to sea was all about, I was sent out to Bombay on Cunard's trooper

Samaria. From Bombay I crossed to Calcutta by train, a very interesting journey but very dusty: it was before the days of air conditioned comfort. We arrived in Calcutta to find it in the grip of that tragic civil war, of Hindus against Muslims. We were smuggled on to a ship in the river close by to wait for things to cool off. I then joined *Orna*, a motorship of 6,779 tons.

The old pattern of trading was now never really to return properly except for a short time. We did several voyages to Rangoon as though we were on the Rangoon mail run, but there was no mail and no passengers. We arrived back in Calcutta on one voyage to find that the pattern had changed. Now we were to load for Australia via Fiji. Pre-war Indian labour had been sent to Fiji to work on the sugar plantations and now we were to take some there and to bring some back. Because *Orna* was a cargo ship, they would have to be carried in the between decks, which they did not like too much as some of them were far from coolie class. All in all, though, we had no trouble after they got used to the idea. To take their minds off of the subject, I organised a concert each way, which was quite successful.

Suva was a nice place and we used to get one night there each way. We carried on to Sydney where we discharged all of our cargo and loaded back with Australian products for Singapore and Calcutta. Dock labour was in very short supply at this time with the result that we stayed about a month in port each time and as a result we got to know a lot of people.

We did several of these voyages, but on one voyage we went to the West Indies instead, to bring back a lot of old people, who had been in Trinidad on the sugar plantations, whose one desire was to return to India before they died. We loaded gunnies as usual for the voyage, discharging in several Cuban ports including Havana. We went via Durban and the South Atlantic. As we approached the North Brazilian coast the weather deteriorated and became rainy. What had happened to the sunny Caribbean? I asked. On approach to Cuba, however, the weather improved.

We went to Trinidad to load some ballast for the voyage back as there was no cargo. We managed to get alongside on New Year's Eve and had a whale of a time. I was taken to the British Club and seemed to drift from party to party, eventually being taken back to my ship at 5 am in reasonably good shape by a doctor from Hong Kong. As most of our passengers were elderly, a doctor was placed in charge of them. Unfortunately, he thought he was in charge of the ship and it was some time before he was persuaded that the captain was in charge of everything. Once this was sorted out, things went smoothly. We picked up passengers in Georgetown, British Guiana, where I met some delightful local people. Out of the 350 passengers, we only lost two or three on the way back.

It was during the course of one of the Fijian voyages that the partition of India took place. We had both Hindus and Muslims in the crew, but there was never any trouble between them. We held a celebration on board with speeches and both sides were more friendly than their governments ever are.

Leave was due again, and I was despatched to Africa to join *Padana* for the voyage to the UK. Another train journey across India, but this time in air conditioned comfort to Bombay where I joined a passenger ship to Mombasa. I found that my ship was in Tanga the next port down, so was flown there in a tiny plane, carrying about eight a side, quite a thrilling experience. The *Padana*, grossing 7,541 tons, was built in 1945 and like many of the company's ships built at this time she was a flush deck ship with three hatches forward and two aft; quite comfortable, though. When we got home, I stayed with her throughout discharge and part loading. For a change, I was to have six months summer and autumn leave.

In due course, one November morning when the thought of returning east was not too bad, I received a letter from the company telling me to stand by for a new ship building on the Clyde in Glasgow. She was the *Chandpara* of 7,273 tons. I joined her on the 1st December and had three weeks to store her and do the hundred and one things necessary before she went on her trials. I was living in a hotel; it was dark when I left in the morning and dark before I left the ship in the afternoon. At last we were ready to go on the berth to load so we made our way around to Middlesborough, my most favourite port, where we started loading for Calcutta. Like her sisters, at 12½ knots she was somewhat faster than the older ships and besides having good accommodation, we had a freezer in which to keep our food instead of the old ice boxes.

At Calcutta we found that we were going on the Australia run. In fact, I had fifteen months on this run and made more friends. During this time I had the luck to be involved in a salvage operation. An Italian passenger liner, *Liguria*, had broken down a few hundred miles from Freemantle. We were the nearest ship so we went to her assistance and towed her to Freemantle, which turned out to be a profitable venture.

Promotion in our company was always by seniority with which I agree, as it prevents a lot of in-fighting and makes for friendly relations. The year was 1950, 24 years after joining the company as an officer. Normally I would have expected command in 16 years, but the war had upset this. I knew by now that I was very close to the top. In Sydney we met *Canara*, whose captain, I knew, was going to retire upon his return to the UK. If I were chief officer of that ship I could see myself taking his place. Her chief officer was willing to exchange and so with wires red hot, the company agreed to the exchange. Later I learned that I would have been promoted on arrival back in Calcutta anyway, but the ship that I would have commanded would not have been the same and I think I made a wise decision.

The expected happened and there I was, with my name on a ship's register for the first time. We had good pursers in B.I. who knew their paperwork backwards and with the help of shore officials, the first unknown moments were steered through. Once we had dropped the pilot, I was thoroughly at home – that's what going to sea is all about. Monarch of all you survey, although not so much these days when the radio telephone call from the owners can wake you up in the middle of the night. This first voyage was to Malta and Port Said to discharge Government stores and then to Savona, in Italy to load rice for the UK. This was a very unusual voyage on which to be thrown in at the deep end.

Back in London, I went on leave and afterwards was flown out to Bombay and sent down to Colombo on P & O's *Chusan*, to join *Mtwara*. She was a small ship built in 1951 for the East Africa feeder service in connection with the ill-fated ground-nut scheme and was an equal dead loss. She was laid-up in Colombo when I joined her but eventually we went to Calcutta to run between Calcutta and Rangoon. Eventually I was moved to *Itaura*, in which I served for some time trading around the Indian coast before eventually I took her home. By now my daughter was old enough to live by herself at home and so my wife and I returned as passengers to Bombay on P & O's new passenger liner *Arcadia*. We had on board the chairman, Sir William Currie, for the voyage as far as Aden.

At Bombay I was appointed to *Olinda*, 5,424 tons, built in 1950. She was sailing from the Persian Gulf to Japan via some twenty ports, a run that used to belong to P & O before the war. I thoroughly enjoyed it, although I did not see much of my wife in Bombay. We went to Shanghai in Communist China, arriving off the port during the night. I thought that I would put on my full uniform and it was just as well that I did because the pilot came on board with more gold braid than I had! Shanghai had changed quite a lot from my first visit. The British Club, which was reputed to have the longest bar in the world, had become a Seamen's Club. There was not a lot for sale in the shops as far as I could see. I was taken out to dinner by the Chinese agents. We had many courses, of I don't know what.

One voyage we went to Taku Bar in the Yellow Sea, the port for Tiensin. There was thick fog all the way in the Yellow Sea, but radar and echo sounder saw me there safely. At Taku Bar I was taken by our Chinese agent to go to the theatre and stay for the night in a hotel. It was an interesting programnme with a warlike overtone. During the interval we went into the vestibule and were surrounded by the audience who were very interested and friendly. I walked around a bit in the morning and, as far as I could see, was not followed by the secret police.

Japan was as interesting as ever, even though a war had taken place since I was last there. It had modernised considerably but there was still a lot of old Japan about. I had more salvage experience while on this run: one of our ships had broken down off the Kathiwar coast in North West India, and as the sou' west monsoon was still blowing, she was in danger of dragging her anchor and going ashore. It was now that my previous experience was so invaluable, not only in knowing what to do, but also dealing with the paperwork involved. I towed her back safely to Bombay amidst a nice lot of congratulatory messages and, later, financial reward. As they say, money for old rope; people ashore always want to buy your old ropes.

And so life continued. There were long delays, usually owing to congested harbours at the top end of the Gulf at Basra and Kharromshahr. It was exceedingly hot, laying at anchor for days on end in the river with no air conditioning in the ship. At last, though, it was time for home leave again and I found myself appointed to take *Palikonda* home. While I was at home this time, my daughter got herself married so this left my wife free to come out to India for my next spell. I was appointed to *Canara* in Bahrain on her way to Australia, which was a run that the company was building up. Ordinarily I would have been very pleased with this, but not this time, as my wife was in Bombay. I managed, however, to get myself transferred in Galle to *Warora*. This was one of a pair of ships of 3,668 gross tons built in 1948, with two hatches forward and two aft with a connecting between deck in Numbers 2 and 3 Holds. Would you believe it, I found myself on the Far East run again, this time returning to Calcutta.

It was in Kobe that I had the dreaded experience of a fire on board. Fortunately, it was in port at Kobe and, owing to the chief officer doing all the right sort of things and the speed with which the stevedores battened down the hatches in order to starve the fire of oxygen, we managed to win out. First of all we smothered the fire with steam and then injected CO_2. This extinguishing system was being fitted in Calcutta but was not completely finished; we made do, though. I did not make the mistake of opening the hatches too soon, which would have renewed the air supply and even when we did open up, it started smouldering again but we had the fire service standing by, and that was that. We never found out the cause of the fire as we could not find the seat when we discharged the cargo. The port authorities and fire service showed their sympathy by showering us with cases of beer. What a good idea! A party was held on board for one and all and a great deal of goodwill was created.

After a while we were taken off this run and were sent to pioneer a new run from the Persian Gulf to East Africa. This was no good to me with a wife in India, so I managed to get myself transferred to *Ordia* and found myself back on the Persian Gulf – Far East run again. Leave became due again, and afterwards we returned to India where I was appointed to *Padana*. They were really quite pleasant ships to be on.

An early voyage was to Rangoon with coal then on to Mauritius with rice, then over to East Africa for cashew nuts for Cochin on the west coast of India. By now wives were able to accompany their husbands for one voyage a year and so my wife came with me on this trip. At Mauritius the agent loaned us a car and we saw quite a lot of the island. Lindi in Tanganyka was our first loading port. It was an anchorage port at the mouth of a river and quite a small place where one could hear lions roaring at night. It had a club on the beach which welcomed us as the few Europeans there were pleased to see a new face. Talking about lions, we were told by a nurse that one had walked right through the hospital one night!

Loading proceeded in daytime at a leisurely pace. A favourite pastime was walking along the beach to see what shells had been cast up as by now my wife had become engrossed in enlarging her collection of them. Mozambique Island was our next port of call. I remember it being a very clean place. I was there once for a New Year's party with our Portuguese agent and, although very little English was spoken, it was very enjoyable.

Eventually, we came to Zanzibar where we filled up with fresh water which came underground from Mount Kilimanjaro, and it was very fresh and plentiful, unlike supplies elsewhere. Then on to Mombasa to fill up and thence to Cochin to discharge. I continued on the Cochin – East Africa cashew nut run for some time, while my wife stayed in Bombay and flew to Cochin while I was in port there. We became very good friends with the agent there; Cochin was known to most captains as the place where it was easier to get beer than fresh water, and that was difficult, too. The agent was forever saying, "I'll try to get some from the Navy." Happy days away from Head Office.

One day, to my surprise, I was transferred to the *Aronda*. She was one of the three built just before the war for the Calcutta – Rangoon mail run. This time, she was connecting the two wings of Pakistan, that is, Chittagong in the East to Karachi in the West. And on that ship I was destined to stay until I retired.

We spent about a week at both ports, calling at Colombo both ways for fuel, water and stores. My wife was living in Bombay and flew to Karachi each time I came, as living in Karachi is not very pleasant. While at Chittagong, the week was fully occupied going to parties as there was nothing else to do. This was too good to last as the Pakistanis brought out a new ship, the *Shams*, to take over. *Aronda* had taken a great part in the history of the two wings of Pakistan so there were official and private parties as we left the run for the last time. We went on to the Bombay – East Africa run after this, and at last I heard that I was going to be relieved at Mombasa on my way back from Durban.

I had made up my mind to retire at 55, only two years short of the maximum age; by now I knew a few people on the East African coast so there were some good-bye parties, too. In a way I was sad to be going, as I had enjoyed my time in the company; I had been to many places and made many friends, and had innumerable acquaintances whom I would miss. At last we reached Mombasa and tied up without mishap and I rang down my last "Finished With Engines". At my last-night party, the officers of all sections of *Aronda* presented me with a silver-plated salver, teapot, hot-water jug, milk jug and sugar bowl. It was suitably inscribed and was a very handsome present, which is in frequent use at home.

On the morning of the 4th April, 1961, I handed over to a very old friend of mine, and as *Aronda* left Mombasa I waved good-bye to her from the bedroom window of my hotel which overlooked the harbour.

Norman Lucas retired from the sea in the twilight of the Merchant Navy's greatness. As he said himself,

How was I to know of the great change that was to take place, all to be under the P & O houseflag, and then containerisation? I must mention, of course, the troopers, which the older inhabitants of Southampton knew well for many years through seeing them laid up off Netley during the off-season in trooping. With the gradual ebbing of this work, the company had to think of new ideas to get a financial return and ships like the *Nevasa* and *Uganda* became famous carrying schoolchildren on educational cruises. *Nevasa* became too expensive to operate, eventually but the Uganda made a maginficent swansong in true B.I. tradition, in the Falklands War.

So ends the story of Norman Lucas and his company, British India, for the last ship to carry the company's House Colours, the *Uganda*, was sold for scrapping in 1986. Perhaps ironically, she was caught by Cyclone Wayne and lay on her side at her anchorage, determined to sell herself dearly.

WATTS WATTS – TRAMPING WITH THE BOATSTEERER

The Boatsteerer is the most vital man in the Club and Captain Ralph Stephenson OBE is constantly occupied; hardly retirement, although Ralph's efficiency makes it look easy. One of nature's gentlemen, Ralph's modesty belies his achievements. He is one of that rare, august breed holding an Extra-Master's Certificate, an élite distinction. As Principal Inspector at the Board of Trade with heavy responsibility for supervising the safety of vessels visiting Southampton, it was a prestigious appointment which necessitated having an Extra-Master's Certificate but at the time it meant a drop in salary of £2,000, which forced Ralph to tighten his belt even harder for he was not paid during the period when he studied for his Extra-Master's: and bear in mind that this was before the war. The highest degree of efficiency was needed and many senior Cachalots recall his examining them in Liverpool and Southampton.

Ralph's sea career started in the Great Depression when he earned his service with one of the leading British companies in the Merchant Navy: not a line of opulent liners but a company of hard-working tramps steaming across the oceans. This was Watts, Watts and Company.

Edmund Watts and William Milburn founded their shipping business in 1857. Realising that the days of sailing ships were numbered, they had visions of establishing a fast steamship service in the lucrative China tea trade. When Milburn, formerly a butcher, decided to concentrate on the carriage of refrigerated meat from Australia to England in 1872 he left the Watts

Company to form his own business, that established the Port Line. Edmund Watts' business flourished in its own right, though and Milburn's place was readily taken by a Mr Ward.

Watts Ward and Company was a London partnership that made its success in cargo tramping in the Victorian age when Britain spawned the greatest deep sea merchant fleet that the world has seen. As modest-sized cargo steamers plied the seas on shoe-string

The "Tottenham" on which Ralph Stephenson served as Chief Officer

budgets, scraping profits on any cargoes that they could secure, they developed principles of shipping upon which so much of the economics of shipping today are based. These tough, unglamorous ships earned the nickname 'tramps' for their often vagrant appearance, unpainted for want of a profit margin and while securing employment for thousands of seafarers the conditions on board often were the most Spartan imaginable, squeezing every penny for profits.

In common with so many shipping operations, the business was run in this way: the Britain Steamship Company was incorporated and registered on the 8th December 1884, and they owned the ships but the task of operating them was managed by the partnership business (that was renamed Watts Watts and Company on Ward's death). In this way the assets (and long-term liabilities like mortgages) were held separate from the business that paid the bills and managed the trading account. To a large extent this business practice prevails today, with ships being owned by a company that takes no part in the management of those vessels.

Sea power and commerce were the guiding lights of the enormous Victorian work ethic and like all British shipping companies, Watts Watts worked feverishly hard, struggling through periodic recessions and tight budgets to win an enviable reputation high in the league of tramping businesses. By the end of the century, the fleet comprised twenty two cargo steamers, many built by Ropner and Son and over the succeeding years they became well-known for maintaining their ships, larger than average, to a most respected standard, named after London suburbs like Twickenham and Greenwich. Moreover, conditions for seafarers in Watts Watts ships were envied by their colleagues serving with rival companies; this extremely praiseworthy practice was to continue as long as the company owned vessels.

Ralph Stephenson served with the company in the years before the Second World War and recalls that the cap badge was surmounted by a crown, as they had a Government contract, for the management of Khedivial Mail, a prestigious achievement for a company basically known for tramping. Still, Ralph well recalls the rigours of seafaring in those days, when as a cadet his badly gashed hand was simply bandaged and he was sent straight back on duty; no sick-leave or repatriation!

Ralph regularly visited Russian ports, where their cargo would be handled by convicts, some of them women, a hard, desperate job especially in the bitter cold. They would deliver machine parts to the Russian ports and collect cargoes of timber, although the shortcomings in Stalin's administration sometimes hardly seemed to be worth their efforts. On one occasion they landed a heavy piece of factory machinery on the dockside with the ship's own lifting gear but there was no dockside crane available, and on his next visit Ralph was surprised to see that the machinery was still lying on the dockside.

In those days there were two kinds of rouble, one of which was a tourist currency which was forbidden to Russian people who had to make do with the local rouble of many times less value. It was a serious offence for visitors to sell their hard roubles to a local and when as a cadet Ralph was caught doing just that, he was arrested and the authorities imposed a fine equivalent to six months pay for Ralph, but eventually they were persuaded to let him off. Before sailing, the ship's company always had to present themselves on deck while the ship was searched for stowaways seeking freedom from starvation and Stalin's iron grip on that great country.

The fleet of Watts Watts had grown to 39 vessels in 1929 but the Depression bit deeply into cargo volumes and freight rates, and by 1934 the company was operating just ten ships. Even in those hard times, though, Ralph recalls that the company still cared for their seafarers, with comforts unknown to other owners. Safety was a priority, aswell, and Watts Watts ordered the first British tramps to be fitted with echo-sounders. Even so, one should not forget that the company's hard-working, coal-burning tramps had to struggle to make a living – and struggling in more ways than one. Ralph's ship was on a two-year charter to a Japanese company when the ship's name was changed to accord with Japanese practice adding 'Maru' after her name, like the *Beckenham Maru*. The heavy Pacific swell was notorious and slowed the ship down dramatically, which was a serious matter for a coal-burning ship with low bunkers. On occasions the ship would be two weeks late because of the swell; they tried navigating every direction to avoid the swell but never did manage to avoid it – such was the problem with the low-power cargo ships of those days. On the documentation the Japanese would state the time fixed for arrival but the ships became so dramatically late that eventually the Japanese did not bother to fill in the arrival fixture at all!

Then, just as things were looking brighter, the Second World War struck. Of the pre-war fleet of nine modern ships, seven were destroyed by enemy action and although eight were built between 1940 and 1944, three of those were lost aswell. For all the losses suffered by the company, their seafarers showed great courage and they earned six OBE's, three Lloyd's Medals, three MBE's, two BEM's and several officers were specially commended. Even the chairman of the board, Edmund Hannay Watts and his wife made a vital contribution to the war effort through the Merchant Navy Comforts Service, a tradition of care for which Watts Watts was famous. Hitler's plans hinged on the fact that British shipping was the one thing which secured the survival of this island race and the sacrfice of so many merchant seafarers stands testimony to their bravery and determination. No where is this better told than in the story of the *Willesden*.

Captain R D Griffiths had already won the OBE when in the spring of 1942 he was in command of the *Willesden* en route from New York to Alexandria via St Thomas. On the 1st April at 5.20 pm a seaplane was spotted 400 feet away approaching from the port side. They were relieved to see that the plane was carrying American markings when it flew straight for them and opened fire on the bridge and on the bofors gun aft, injuring the gun's crew and putting it out of action. The plane dropped a bomb which fell 200 feet short and by a trailing hook, carried away the ship's aerial as it flew over. A few minutes later a ship was spotted approaching on the port quarter about eight miles distant. The *Willesden* then came under fire from 5-gun and 3-gun salvoes from this raider, one shell striking the No 2 hatch and deck, setting fire to the dangerous deck cargo of 60-gallon drums of aircraft fuel. The second shell struck the lower bridge, killing the bosun as well as some crew who were lowering a lifeboat and wounded the second officer.

The fire was burning fiercely now and the captain decided to abandon ship. While this was going on, some of the men bravely engaged the raider with the 4-inch gun. Disappointingly, though the range was too great and the shells fell short. The captain ordered the confidential papers to be taken to the stokehold and burned, when the third shell struck the port side on the waterline, causing some plates to leak and the fourth shell struck the starboard lifeboat forward davit, following which a rating later died of his wounds.

At 6.00 pm the captain gave the order to abandon ship and the survivors were picked up by the German raider whose commander congratulated Captain Griffiths and his ship's company for their splendid resistance. Trouble times lay ahead for the men, though, for they were taken to a Japanese prison camp. On their release, the captain, chief officer and chief engineer were all recognised in awards.

Following the end of the war the company struggled on with seven ships but new tonnage was ordered in 1946, beginning a gradual rebuilding programme that followed an upward trend in their fortunes. Fleet losses would not be the only problem to be faced now, though. The post-war period saw a change in trading patterns which had a massive effect on the long-term future of British deep sea shipping, as emergent nations fought to secure larger shares of their markets and their marine trades for themselves and the cost of employing European crews rose alarmingly.

For some years, though, Watts Watts looked good. New tonnage, the *Wanstead* and her successors, boasted excellent crew accommodation and the leading technical designs in the tramping industry – and the ships were making money. In 1954 the issued share capital stood at £1 million and the fleet cost on the books stood at £3,147,310. A very acceptable dividend was returned of 10 per cent and in the following year this increased to 15 per cent. By 1956 the company's performance justified further fleet expansion and the issued share capital was increased to £2½ million, with the fleet at cost on the books now at £4,057,000. By the end of that year, though, the dividend fell to 12 per cent. In 1957 the fleet increased still further but the dividend declared remained at 12 per cent. In 1958 the fleet cost was increased to £5,612,150 but for the first time the dividend declared was nil. Still, with no mortgages to pay on the ships, the company had the resilience to absorb financial blows, with a fleet of ten ships totalling 64,109 tons and an average age of eight years. That resilience was needed, though, for by the end of 1960, with a fleet of eight ships averaging 7,300 tons and five years apiece, the company had made a trading loss of £342,352 over the year.

This marked the point where the influences on British shipping began to bite and in 1962 the trading loss was £380,192. In the same year, Edmund Watts died and although at the time the company was busy with its own fleet aswell as managing seven Gulf Oil tankers, massive losses followed before they staged a heroic struggle to make a trading profit of £2,857 in 1965. In that year they were admitted to the Seabridge consortium and an order was placed for a 75,000 deadweight tonnes bulk carrier, following the latest trends of the economies of scale that transformed the face of tramping with massive vessels that grew ever larger as technology permitted, offering new advantages in the Parcel Size Distribution Function. This all gladdened the optimists but the forces at work had a strangle-hold on the Red Duster. These forces were identified as being seven-fold:

1. The collapse of the British Empire and its protected trade.
2. The struggle for maritime emancipation by emergent nations, to protect and encourage their own merchant fleets.
3. The desire by many countries to subsidise their shipping industries as a means of obtaining hard foreign currency.
4. Social reforms at home which brought a massive escalation in British crewing costs.
5. A reduction in the import of bulk raw materials as developing countries learned to process their own resources and the swift move away from Britain as the workshop of the world.
6. Changes in the methods of cargo handling and in the commodities offered for shipment by sea; notably the container and the aeroplane.
7. The introduction of instantaneous global communications.

Watts Watts' accountants reported that as at the 31st December 1966 the company had made a trading loss for the year, this time £19,431, a bitter disappointment for this fine company and no doubt the board of directors had to consider very hard the prospect that they had done all that they could; it was a question of finding the money to survive, to pay for adapting to the modern shipping trends that had resulted from the post-war forces on the industry. But the money could not be found and like so many fine British companies, they had to accept that, on present trends, in time their debts would outstrip their assets and they would be insolvent.

The Britain Steamship Company of Watts Watts and Company Limited had considerable goodwill, though, and complete extinction was averted when in 1968 the entire shareholding was purchased by the Bibby Line who absorbed the Britain Steamship Company into their own operation and Watts Watts and Company was wound up, in the same year in which Bibby broke new ground and started their successful gas carrier charter fleet. Bibby later transferred handy-sized bulkships to the company's name, but the highly-respected house of Watts Watts was lost. Bibby have continued to own ships since then and, like an echo, some of them have been registered in the name of the Britain Steamship Company.

GORDON RENSHAWE OF THE NAVVIES

During the Napoleonic Wars, Britian's exports increased by nearly 300 per cent, consisting largely of cotton and iron products aswell as wool. British merchant traders therefore learned the art of international trade but foreign customers gradually developed their own industries and so demand was reduced, which put a lot of British workers out of a job, a dangerous factor in a post-war climate where there were large numbers of unemployed sailors and soldiers cooling their heels. By the early years of the 1820's the country was heavily in debt with high taxation, higher prices and a depreciated currency, all against a background of political unrest. To make matters worse, newly-liberated South American countries made dazzling investment offers but then crashed with their investors' money. Overpopulation in large towns was giving special cause for concern because of the political climate and so in 1824 the Government announced that it would give grants to aid emigration and thousands of people went to South Africa and Canada.

Amid this highly unfavourable background, of which Dickens would have much to say, a group of businessmen were forming a plan. Mr William Hall was a shipowner who had vessels trading between London and Hull. Mr Thomas Brocklebank was a wealthy timber merchant who owned the *Eagle*, a paddle steamer operating between London and Margate. These two men were the force behind an association with nine others who decided to form a company to develop steam navigation with plans to trade to India, North and South America, Portugal, Spain, France, Holland and Russia. In fact their trade would be limited, from London to Hamburg and Brest and subsequently to the

Mediterranean, but that company, affectionately known as the Navvies, would become virtually a household name after its formation on the 11th June 1824 as the General Steam Navigation Comapany Limited.

Their success earned them early rewards and by 1837 they owned forty steamers on services between British and Continental ports. The steamer now was overhauling the sailing ship for speed and reliability and General Steam's ships won a reputation for excellence that became a tradition, whether they be paddle steamers like the *Leith*, a wooden vessel of 907 gross tons built in 1837 or impressive screw ships like the *Halcyon*, 1,566 tons, built in 1921.

The world developed great ocean trades, but the Navvies were more than content with their prospects and their ships mostly on home trades, where they reached pre-eminence. They progressed, therefore, to the point where they would be a very attractive business acquisition for a larger organisation that saw how General Steam could benefit their own Balance Sheets.

So it was, in 1920, that the Peninsular and Oriental Steam Navigation Company acquired the controlling interest in General Steam. In fact, this favoured the Navvies well and under P and O's guidance they would eventually control some eighty subsidiaries. The Navvies continued to reign supreme on short sea routes and they followed a policy of co-operation between various interests engaged in similar trades and also co-ordinated various shipping services rather than face cut-throat competition. The results were economies in operation which benefitted the shipper, who was assured of regular sailings and prompt attention to requirements, as well as as the owners and their shareholders.

This gives just the essential background of one of the most beloved of shipping companies, in which one of Southampton Master Mariners' Club's great characters held a Foreign-Going Master's Certificate. Gordon Renshawe is a great raconteur and every inch a 'Navvie'; here is his own account of life in General Steam:

General Steam's houseflag was a red world on a white background, with the letters G S N C in each corner, and under the orb the date 1824. The company motto was 'Semper Fidelis':

'Always Faithful', but they were affectionately known as 'Generally Slow, Never Certain'! Throughout all the years of their life General Steam were innovative and adventurous. Although essentually short sea traders, in two world wars their vessels and masters sailed to all parts of the world. The sea-going certificates required were Foreign Going, although there were also some certificated officers with Home Trade qualifications. During their time, General Steam directors were big men in the shipping industry, the Brocklebanks, Inchcapes and Andersons.

Passenger ships sailed from London to Leith, Bordeaux and Portugal, but we must not forget the famous 'Eagle' paddle steamers on the Thames, taking thousands of Cockneys on what, for some, was their only holiday in the year, to Southend, Margate and Clacton. There were regular cargo runs to North Europe, Iberia and the Mediterranean. Most of the London cargo operations were at one time based at St Katherine's or Brewers Quay in the Pool of London aswell as at the nearby buoys. The Head Office was first in Leadenhall Street, perhaps the most famous street in world shipping, and then at 15 Trinity Square, before moving to a site alongside the Tower of London in 1960, on their bombed-out cargo wharfs, called Three Quays.

One of Lord Nelson's captains, Captain Lilliot, later to found Royal Mail, chartered a ship to serve in the War of the Portuguese Succession, in which he sailed as supercargo and his letter of appreciation still exists in Oporto. Royalty were not unknown to General Steam in the early days. Queen Victoria and Prince Albert were interested in the new developments of the Age, and the Queen was so seasick on the outward trip of her first voyage to Scotland in the sail-powered *Royal George* that, on seeing a General Steam vessel in Leith harbour, she chartered her for the return, arriving in state and comfort less than three days later. This was commemorated until the end of the company's identity by its white lifeboats having a purple band painted around them.

The company expected all employees to use their initiative, especially in the days before good communications, and this coupled with economic conditions produced individuals of great character and independance, with firm convictions, right or wrong, aswell as some eccentrics whose feats of semanship or otherwise would today provide several exciting scripts for television. The company directors in my time were somewhat aloof except for the twice yearly dance at Bush House, when all sea and shore staff available were invited and danced, mixing freely with glass in hand. An enthusiastic dancer from the lower orders was often worried about his promotion prospects after pounding the toes of a director's wife.

One director, Percy Privitt, having been trapped as Manager in Hamburg at the start of the Great War, spent the whole war in a prisoner of war camp. The camp was for merchant seamen captured at sea, and he organised and encouraged all types of sports and studies and several did indeed pass their professional certificates for use after the war. When he became a director, he always thought so highly of the sea staff that he stood up for them, as shore staff rather looked down upon the seafarers. During the Second World War he insisted on building the coaster *Kingfisher*, the first to be built in which each rating had his own cabin.

Percy's trade mark was a bright red, bulbous nose. He once noticed a passing second mate glancing at this conspicuous beacon and remarked, "When your yearly salary, young man, equals the sum needed to maintain this luminosity, you will be in a position to marry", a hint to study harder for the required master's ticket. He used to hold court in the nearby 'Cheshire Cheese' under Fenchurch Street railway arches every lunch time.

Often he would telephone a lowly member of the Port of London Authority staff, or some other organisation with whom they needed to keep in good favour, such as a foreman in a warehouse in Surrey Docks, and say, "You mean bugger, you haven't bought me a G and T lately." The foreman would say proudly to his mates, "I'm going Up City to buy old Percy a drink, he's a director of General Steam, you know." The drink would be accepted, but the rest of the session and the sandwiches would be on 'P.P.', with lots of chaffing, but no mention of favours required. Should a hold-up to discharge or some other problem occur in that area later, P.P. would jokingly ask what was happening: problem solved right away. After he died, in a similar situation, after pleadings from the ship's officers the company would send down a young clerk with five pounds in an envelope. But this was regarded as a bribe, and not the slightest notice was taken of such an impersonal gesture.

The Thames Watermen and Lightermen, who acted as Mud (Dock) Pilots from time immemorial, each jealously guarded their own section of the river and usually employed their own sons as boatmen, while also tying up the vessel at the river and dock berths. The families went back many generations and had a great pride in the history and traditions of the river, but above all they had a tremendous sense of humour. A meeting for business reasons at a frontier pub between the heads of two families was not for the faint hearted. The conversation was conducted at full blast, over many pints, and the profanities and expletives of their normal conversation would have brought business to a juddering halt around any City pub, but went unnoticed even by the stout grey-haired ladies behind the bar.

George Baker and his three sons of Surrey Dock were one such family. George was famous for his heart of gold, his generosity and his oft-stated boast that the Watermen's Company was founded years before Trinity House in Stuart times, aswell as for his vocabulary that did indeed uphold riverside traditions. He once asked me to inquire tactfully of the Surrey Dock harbour master why he had not been invited to a Trinity House annual reception that summer. The harbour master, who was a Younger Brother of Trinity House, reported that the year before, the guest of honour had been the Master of Trinity House, the then Duke of Gloucester, who in conversation with the harbour master inquired, "I suppose, Harbour Master, in the course of your duties you meet many of OUR pilots while they are berthing the ships in your docks?" The harbour master explained that the Trinity House pilots took the ships into the locks, but the ships were berthed by a Waterman. The Duke was surprised and suggested that the job would be done better by a "proper pilot". Big, burley George, in his best suit, overheard this; he grabbed the Duke by his lapels and bellowed, "You old ****, you know **** all."

In the last years of the company, they built the fourth and largest *Eagle* for the Southampton – Lisbon – Tangier weekly ferry run, carrying over 720 passengers and many cars aswell as freight in lorries and containers. This run required that a doctor be carried together with a fully-equipped hospital. Dr Ernest Winters, who was a sea fanatic, ran a large practice in Harrow and offered to staff the ship in this respect. One of his partners came each week, but he came at least once a month himself. He was rotund and jolly with an infectious laugh; he was also very tactful and was immensely popular, solving many personal and family problems of the ship's company, with a quiet chat on his walks around the ship.

When not in his surgery, or on his rounds to seasick passengers, he was to be found on the bridge, with a huge pair of binoculars slung around his neck; he was far more effective than the official A.B. lookout, such was his keenness. He always made the Christmas trip and had a Santa Claus outfit tailor-made in the West End aswell as a sledge made by the ship's carpenter. He loved children and on Christmas Day, the sledge was pulled into the main Red Room lounge by stewards. This impressive saloon with fine decor ran almost a third of the length and half the breadth of the ship. On these occasions it was filled with excited children and the hostess ensured that the arrival of Father Christmas was the highlight of the day. The noise on the appearance of a jolly, red-faced Santa atop his sleigh, with a sack-full of gifts, must have shocked the lighthouse keeper on distant Ushant.

One Christmas, the company decided to have a comic Neptune instead, giving out gifts alongside the swimming pool bar. They chose a pompous, ex-Cunard purser of enormous proportions, who surprisingly quite liked the idea and refused to step down in favour of the old procedure at the suggestions of the sea staff. He was to be attired in a jacket apparently made of old saucepan lids, and a seaweed skirt. This surly apparition, with his fat legs and girth, would have put fear into the Ship's Company, let alone the terrified youngsters. Ernest was very hurt, but pretended that he did not expect to be Father Christmas every year. The vessel sailed two days before Christmas, but early on Christmas morning, the purser, perhaps having a hangover, foolishly went up to the surgery and asked Ernest for some aspirin. He was immediately clapped into the two-berth hospital cabin, the most awful diseases suspected. He was finally released the morning after, only after the children and staff had enjoyed an unusually ebullient traditional party with Ernest as Santa distributing the presents. Ernest, by a strange coincidence, had brought his outfit anyway.

It must be admitted that on regular Continental cargo runs, a more amusing and pleasurable liaison was set up with local ladies of the cafés than was to be found in legal domesticity at home in London. Bordeaux and Hamburg were especially famous between the wars for exciting relationships. The Marine Department tactfully never forwarded to the home address letters and messages arriving from abroad for crew members, but kept them to be collected personally. Several masters had girlfriends in Hamburg and when they were not required on board, they would stay with them for a couple of days (and nights) a week. Two had long-term girlfriends, known affectionately to the crews as 'Bunker ****' and 'Gold Tooth Annie'. Fifteen years after the war I met Gold Tooth Annie again. She was now a plump, elderly lady and when I asked her about her nickname, for she was now wearing a perfect set of dentures with no sign of gold adornment, she replied, "Oh, the Nazis took it in the war, but my Alfred still likes me." The gentleman concerned, within weeks of retirement, nodded agreement.

The inevitable end came for the company with the anonymity of computers, takeovers and hatchet jobs, and so finished one hundred and fifty years of adventure, business acumen, superb seamanship, wartime heroics and, above all, of comradeship, kindliness and humour. Fading memories now, but in their time a sturdy body of patriotic men and women who contributed much to the maritime glory of which our country was once so proud.

I heard of the Southampton Master Mariners' Club in the early 'fifties, when, inward bound from Tonnay Charante with brandy, our small vessel of 500-odd tons thumped the Town Pier rather hard. The pilot was most annoyed, as his previous job had been the *Queen Mary*, so he promised the Old Man he would atone for the dent by buying him a pint at the Club. I was tempted to join the Club in 1965, while relieving on a new 'push-button' coaster of the G.S.N.C. home trade fleet, based in Southampton, sailing twice a week to Le Havre with general cargo. I really began to appreciate the Club more fully, when exiled (but very happily) to Hull for the North Sea Ferries run between Hull and Rotterdam.

I received a letter from the Boatsteerer, Percy Cooper, thanking me for my subscription and giving me all the local news, wondering how I was and assuring me of a noggin on my return. Since then Old 'Nick' and Ralph Stephenson have continued the tradition that makes one feel part of a super crowd of people.

I was delighted to be elected Sea Staff Captain in 1976, which was very convenient as I was then on charter to Truckline sailing between Poole and Cherbourg. I was even more pleased when one Saturday morning in 1985 Captain Stephenson rang me out of the blue and asked me to be Staff Captain and of course in 1987 I was Captain of the Club. I was especially happy to have the Earl of Darnley speaking at my Sea Pie Supper, as he had worked in the port office of P and O Ferries, now lost in Ocean Village.

Captain Charles Worth, a past Captain of the Club, said, "The Club is our own little ship on the shore" and when one thinks of the great fellowship of the Boatsteerers, Officers, Cachalots and fantastic Messmates and their ladies (of such pleasant company) both past and present, I am sure that if 'Fiddlers Green' is anything like the Club, I shall be more than happy there, but not yet, I hope.

RON FREAKER: BLUE STARS, BLUE WHALES

In his superb book, 'Before The Box Boats', Captain A W Kinghorn of the Blue Star Line recalls the captivating yarns from the reefer trade, guaranteed to terrify the cadets, like the tales about rats which live in the numerous narrow tunnels which carry cold air around the holds. Due to those climatic conditions

The famed "Arandora Star", on which Ron Freaker served as 4th Officer

the rats grow luxurious coats like Persian cats.... And the rats live like kings off the cargoes of food and are so fierce that an officer going down a hold to inspect the cargo was attacked and eaten; all that was found were the brass buttons off his jacket....

Many a tale of the Blue Star Line has been recalled over a pint in the Club. It all started when in 1879 two Liverpool brothers, William and Edmund Vestey, went into partnership trading in the meat retail and cold store business. They had no trouble *storing* the meat, but what was increasingly troubling them was how to *bring* it here. They relied entirely on shipping companies transporting the meat from South America in refrigerated ships, for which they had to pay high freight rates that cut their profits. The Vesteys therefore tried to negotiate with the Royal Mail Steam Packet Company for a reduction in the rate for their meat cargoes from Argentina, where most of their meat came from. They could not agree anything with them, though, so they took the most obvious alternative: they decided to go into shipowning themselves, to carry their own cargoes – and anybody else's who could fill spare capacity.

In 1909 they purchased two refrigerated cargo steamers from Shaw, Savill and Albion and on the 28th July 1911, the Blue Star Line Limited was formed. By the end of the First World War there were nine ships in the fleet, five of which were some twenty years old, a hoary old age to fight for profits and so a fleet rebuilding programme was started. By the mid-1920's the company was in good shape and the River Plate trade was attracting Blue Star ships bound homewards with meat cargo. Because the line was outside the South America Freight Conference the ships had to make the outward voyage in ballast when obviously they could not earn money. It would have been ideal if their company could join the conference but its admission was constantly blocked by certain existing conference members and so in reply Blue Star built nine splendid new ships reflecting their exciting confidence in an expansion into passenger work which grandly circumvented the conference's obstruction aswell as increasing cargo work.

The new passenger service commenced in February 1927 when the *Almeda*, the first of the new liners, sailed from London for Buenos Aires via Lisbon, Teneriffe, Rio de Janeiro, Santos and Montevideo and by the end of the year the service was offering fortnightly sailings. The success of these magnificent ships was particularly disagreeable to the Royal Mail Steam Packet Company, headed by Lord Kylsant in those worrying times, whose

Farewell from London: The William Scoresby *Sails for the Antarctic*

The Officers of the William Scoresby: *Ron Freaker is second from the right. The man in civilian dress is the Norwegian "Gunner"*

new diesel-powered liners were proving slower than expected and suffered badly from vibration.

It was this company in which a certain Ronald Clifford Freaker would learn the profession of the sea. Like most Master Mariners, he signed his indentures at the age of sixteen and learned the job in the only way – the hard way. Soon Ron's would prove to be no ordinary service, though, thanks to a ship called the *Arandora Star*. Launched in 1927 for the company's prestige, First Class passenger liner service, the recession in shipping was beginning to bite by the time she was commissioned and made Blue Star consider offering cruises. In January 1929 the liner, originally named *Arandora* was taken out of service and converted into a magnificent cruise ship. Radical internal and superstructure alterations gave her an increased passenger capacity of 400 and she emerged on the 31st May 1929, a truly beautiful ship, soon to have a white hull and carmine red band, and a new name, *Arandora Star*. Destined for a legendary life as the most luxurious cruise ship in the world, she sailed on summer cruises to the norhern capitals, Norway and the North Cape; to the Mediterranean in spring and autumn and while Europe shivered miserably in the depths of winter she made a Christmas cruise to the West Indies and Hawaii. It was befitting that she should have a suitable home, and Blue Star operated her out of Southampton. The *Arandora* Star was now to be Ron's home, where he was 4th Mate, and here he would serve the company with other names who would become close friends over the years in Southampton Master Mariners' Club. But life on board was not going to be a picnic: she was the company's flagship and had a reputation to make, and it became legendary that her master ran the ship's company with the discipline and efficiency of a Royal Naval vessel.

It was to be only a few years, though, before Ron left the opulence of the world's most luxurious cruise ship for a very different sort of adventure. We all look back on our lives and somehow seem to recall one particular period with more relish and affection than others. For Ron, there was no contest: it was his service in the very early days of Antarctic research. He must tell the story in his own words:

Ron Freaker: Blue Stars, Blue Whales

Ron Freaker in Antarctic Waters

Whale marking

The Wake of the Cachalots

During my twenty five years at sea, mainly in the Merchant Service but also as a Royal Naval Reserve officer, I had a very varied career, serving in cargo ships, passsenger liners, a research ship, a cruiser, a seaplane carrier, corvettes and frigates. I believe that I was fortunate indeed to have such varied experience, but to me the most interesting part was the time which I spent in the Royal Research Ship *William Scoresby* during the period 1934 to 1938.

The *William Scoresby* was operated by the 'Discovery' Committee in the 'Discovery Investigations', which were carried out in the interests of the Falkland Islands Dependencies and were concerned with the whaling industry – the main industry of the islanders.

Whaling in the Antarctic began in 1904, when there were enormous numbers of whales in Antarctic waters. In the early days, whale catchers operated from shore stations in the islands of the dependencies. After they were killed the whales were towed to the shore stations by the catchers, where they were hauled up onto a slip or 'plan' and there the blubber was stripped off and the carcass cut up. Later, when the whales were found to be more plentiful in the open ocean further away from the islands, the catchers operated in conjunction with factory ships, which were fitted with a slipway in the stern and a large plan on the upper deck. The carcasses of the dead whales were hauled up the slipway on to the plan and then stripped of blubber and cut up.

The factory ship with a group of catchers was able to stop in a position where whales were found to be plentiful, and the catchers were able to operate in the vicinity and tow the carcasses of the whales they killed to the factory ship. In the period when the *Scoresby* was engaged in whale marking, from 1934 to 1938, there were usually about eight factory ships operating in Antarctic waters and the *Scoresby* was able to replenish from these factory ships when necessary, and thus she was able to remain at sea for the whole of the whaling season, normally from November to March.

I joined the *William Scoresby* as Chief Officer in the autumn of 1934 at the commencement of her fourth commission. She had been built by Cook Walton & Gemmell Limited in 1926 and, as far as I know, was the only ship ever built as a whale-marking vessel. Her length was 128 feet 4 inches between perpendiculars and breadth 26 feet. Net tonnage was 112, gross 324 tons. She had an oil fuel capacity of 145 tons and her triple expansion steam engines gave her a designed maximum speed of 12 knots. She was registered at Port Stanley in the Falkland Islands and on her fourth commission had a total complement of 23, which included a scientist and our Norwegian 'gunner', for marking not killing.

We sailed from London on the 18th October 1934. After a short stay in Cape Town we proceeded south to the edge of the pack ice. We marked our first whales, two Blues and one Fin, on the 1st December, at Latitude approximately 81° S Longitude 29° E., and we sighted our first iceberg on the 2nd December at Lat 53° S Long 30° E. We encountered the edge of the pack ice at about Lat 56° S, Long 30° E on the 3rd December. For the next four months we were to be at sea without sighting land, our main ineterests in life being whales and ice, and it was from this time that I realised how absorbing both these were – but particularly the whales.

Like all seafarers I had previously sighted an occasional whale blowing in the distance but really knew nothing about them, so I started to learn as much as I could about these fascinating creatures. The method of marking the whales was by firing a 10 inch dart from a single barrelled 12 bore rifle, the intention being that the dart would pierce the blubber of the whale and the leaden head would lodge in the flesh of the whale, so that if the whale was caught and the blubber stripped off in factory ship or whaling station, the mark would be found and a reward was offered for the return of the mark together with particulars of the place and date of capture.

In order to mark the whales it was, of course, necessary to get very close to them, in the same way that the whale catchers had to get close in order to fire a harpoon into a whale. For this reason, for my first two commissions in the Scoresby we carried the Norwegian gunner I mentioned above, who had had experience shooting whales with a harpoon gun from a whale catcher.

Life in the old whale catchers was a tough business. When a whale was first sighted, the gunner, who was generally also the captain of the whale catcher, would 'con' the catcher from the bridge until they got fairly close and then he would go forward to the 'gun' on the fo'c'sle head and con the catcher from there until he was able to fire the harpoon into the whale. The harpoon weighed about 150lbs and had an explosive grenade attached. The grenade was set to explode three seconds after the gun was fired – yet apparently it was very seldom that one harpoon would kill the whale; it was generally necessary to fire a second. The dart had 50 metres of $4\frac{1}{2}$ or 5 inch manilla line attached to it, and this was attached to 600 fathoms of 8 inch manilla, so that the whale was able to sound, or dive deep, with the harpoon in its body.

The suffering of these great animals before they finally died does not bear thinking about. In fact, I believe that it has been said that if a whale could scream, no man would have the heart to kill it in this way. Unfortunately for the whale, it cannot scream or make any sound to be heard by its killers. The only evidence is the large area of blood-stained water surrounding the wounded or dead whale. When I learned all this, I was very glad that we were engaged in marking whales and not killing them.

The marking, with our small darts, was unlikely to be felt as anything more than a pin prick, if that, by the whale. I recall with distress, though, that on one occasion, after marking a whale, its 'blow' appeared to be blood-stained, which would seem to indicate that, in this case, the mark had entered the whale's lung. I am glad to say that this was the only occasion when I saw any such evidence.

As I have said, it was from the time when we became engaged in the marking of whales that I realised what interesting creatures they are, and learned as much as I could about them. From reports and other literature that we had on board I discovered that all whales belong to the order 'Cetacea', which is divided into two sub-orders, the Baleen Whales and the Toothed Whales.

Baleen Whales are divided into two families, Rorquals and Right Whales. The family of Rorquals include the Blue, Fin, Sei, Minke and Humpback, and, I believe, the Gray Whale of the North Pacific. The Right Whales include the species of the Southern

Right, the Greenland Whale, Biscay and Black Right (the Nordkaper) aswell as the Pigmy Right.

Toothed Whales are divided into three families:the Sperm (also known as the Cachalot!) and the Pigmy Sperm;the of Bottle Nosed and Beaked Whales; and the 'Delphinadae', which includes the species of Killer or Grampus, Ca'aing, White or Beluga, Narwhal, Common Dolphin, White Beaked Dolphin and the River Dolphins.

Out of all the whales I was most interested in those which were being killed in large numbers in the Antarctic during the years that I was down there marking between 1934 and 1938. These were the Blue, Fin, Humpback and the Sperm. As I have mentioned, Blue, Fin and Humpback are Baleen Whales, which means that they do not have teeth but baleen plates attached to the upper jaw. The Blue has between 250 and 400 baleen plates on each side of its upper jaw. These whales live mainly on krill, a small, shrimp-like creature about 2 1/2 inches long, which is found in enormous quantities in Antarctic waters. When it approaches a shoal of krill, a Baleen Whale has only to open its large lower jaw, and when its mouth is full it closes the lower jaw and the water is forced out between the hundreds of baleen plates attached to the upper jaw. The inside edges of these baleen plates have hairs which prevent the krill from being washed out. The whale then has only to hold its tongue (which in a Blue Whale weighs several tons), to help swallow the krill.

The Blue Whale is the largest of the Baleen Whales and the largest creature which has ever lived on earth. From what I read in 1934, the largest Blue measured by the Discovery expedition was 93 feet 6 inches. This was measured from the tip of the upper jaw to the notch between the flukes, which is the usual method of taking measurement. The overall length, from the tip of the mandible to the tip of the flukes would be about 6 feet longer, so that a total length of 100 feet is quite probable and that of 90 feet not uncommon. According to this report, the majority of females measured between 76 and 88 feet, while the males averaged three or four feet less. For all her enormous size, the female Blue has a gestation period of just 10 1/2 months, after which she delivers a calf nearly 23 feet long, and during a nursing period of six or seven months, the calf grows to a length of about 52 feet.

The Blue would weigh up to 150 tons. The whalers themselves reckoned that these whales weighed a ton per foot; this was probably fairly accurate for whales of average length. I believe that an average elephant, the largest land animal, weighs about three tons, so this should help as some guide to the enormous size of these whales.

Being the largest of them all, the Blue Whales were naturally the greatest prize for the whalers and in the season 1935-'36 10,382 Blue Whales were taken, against 4,824 Fin, 1,254 Humpback and 110 Sperm. Whales were hunted and killed simply for their oil; the average yield was between 70 and 80 barrels, but as much as 305 have been obtained. The whole carcass of the whale, blubber, meat and bones, was boiled down to produce the oil, and of course the quantity of oil produced depended on the size of the whale. For comparison purposes, all the whales caught were reduced to 'Blue Whale Units', so in this way one Blue Whale equalled two Fin Whales, three Humpback and six Sei Whales.

Naturally, the whalers always went after the Blues whenever they were about but in the years 1934 to '38 when we were marking, the Fin Whales were much more numerous than the Blues and the majority of whales which we marked were Fins. Industrial trends were not always for the demand for oil, of course; in the nineteenth century, when ladies wore whalebone corsets, the baleen plates of the whales were the most profitable products. In fact the reason why the Right Whales, which have very much larger baleen plates than the Rorquals, where so-named was because they were the 'right' whales for whalers to catch! I once read that the quantity of baleen, or whalebone, obtained from one Right Whale was enough to pay for the whole cruise of one whaling ship in the nineteenth century.

The Fin Whale was particularly noticeable for the numbers we could see together in a school at any one time. I do not recall seeing more than two or three Blue Whales at any one time, but we frequently saw as many as ten Fin Whales together. On one occasion we saw in the distance a school of about 50 whales blowing, it was an incredible sight. When we got amongst them they seemed to split up into a number of small groups, but they were all Fins.

We also noticed that if we started to chase two or three Fins they would invariably be joined by others, so that we would find ourselves chasing 5 or 6 or even more Fins.

We learned from our Norwegian gunner, and later from our own experiences, that there were two ways of getting close enough to mark a whale. One way was to approach the whale (or whales) at slow speed, being careful not to change the rate of our propeller, for any change in the number of revolutions would invariably be detected by the whales. By this method it was sometimes possible to get within range of the whales, without frightening them.

I well remember, that when the whales were swimming slowly, they would normally blow every two or three minutes, but they were always liable to sound (or dive deep) suddenly, and would stay down for ten to fifteen minutes. We had no idea where they might appear, it might be astern of us at some distance, or, as sometimes happened, right alongside the ship. If we had a good look-out man in the crow's nest he might sight the whale some distance below the surface and warn us – otherwise it could be a frightening experience to hear the roar of the whales blow very close before sighting it. This method of stalking a whale required a lot of patience.

If it was frightened by the sound of the propeller we would increase speed and chase the whale which would then increase its own speed and 'run'. The advantage for us was that the faster a whale runs, the more frequently it has to blow and also the straighter course it keeps, so we had a better chance to mark it. This method was not so effective with the Blues of which we only rarely saw more than two together, and as a Blue is capable of speeds up to 15 knots and our maximum speed was only 12 knots, we could not be sure of catching up with them when they were running – and even after running for some distance they were liable to sound and then appear after ten minutes or so in an unexpected position. If, after chasing Blue whales for two hours we could still not get within range, we would normally end the chase.

The Wake of the Cachalots

With Fin Whales we were usually more successful. We might start chasing two or three Fins and then find ourselves following a school of as many as ten. We were then likely to get within range of some, and often we were able to mark most of them. When running they have to blow frequently, so often five or six Fins would blow at the same time, just ahead of us. The blow of a Fin Whale reaches a height of about twenty feet, so that, standing on the fo'c'sle head of the *Scoresby*, with marking guns in hand we would find ourselves going through a cloud of mist which was the combined blow of 6 or more whales. During these times I learned that Fins can suffer from halitosis!

Another whale which was taken by the whalers in Antarctic waters during the years we were there was the Sperm Whale, the only large Toothed Whale; with an average length of 55 feet, it is smaller than the Baleens, and has a very thick-set head and body, with a single blow-hole at the top of the forehead slightly to the left of centre, unlike the Rorquals which have twin blow-holes in the top of the head.

Sperm Whales are found in all the oceans of the world, in all waters frm Polar ice to the tropics. Moby Dick was a Sperm and indeed the Sperm is also known as the 'Cachalot', so it is a species close to the hearts of the members of the Southampton Master Mariners' Club, whose subtitle is 'The Cachalots', for, according to that writer of sea-stories of the old sailing whalers, the late Mr Bullen, the Cachalot was the species of whale which 'has the thickest skin, blows the hardest and spouts the most'! I told my fellow-Club members that I had seen for myself how every word was true. I have mentioned that the method of marking whales was to fire a dart consisting of a 10 inch stainless steel tubular dart into the whale. This tube had a leaden head with a blunt point, and when marking Baleen whales the mark would always penetrate the outer skin and blubber of the whale either completely or, at most, leaving one or two inches of the dart showing. When we tried marking Sperm Whales, though, we found that the mark usually only penetrated a few inches into the blubber and therefore was likely to be washed out when the whale dived. We solved the problem by sharpening the leaden heads of the darts when we were about to mark Sperm Whales – and I can therefore vouchsafe the truth of what they say about Cachalots!

I have probably said enough about whales to show you what interesting creatures they are; but, in telling of my experiences in the *William Scoresby*, I must also describe that ubiquitous feature of all our commissions: ice. Of all its different forms, I think the most impressive is the iceberg, and of these the most awesome are the tabular bergs, which are only found in Antarctic regions.

Tabular bergs are 'calved' or broken off from the face of the ice barriers which form the coastline in many parts of the continent. The best-known, of course, is the Ross Sea Barrier, made famous from the days of Scott, Shackleton and other, early Antarctic explorers. Most of the tabular bergs seemed to have a height of about 100 feet, but their depth would have been five or six hundred feet.

Many tabular icebergs between 100 yards and a quarter of a mile long can be seen, and there are records of some of enormous sizes, but I well recall the largest one that I saw. We encountered it in the fog when we were steaming north. Due to the very poor visibility we were proceeding at a reduced speed when we sighted a solid wall of ice. It was about 100 feet high as usual, and we had to alter course so turned about 90° to port. We then found that we were steaming parallel to the face of this berg – and we continued to do so for 40 miles! We eventually came to the end of this face, and were able to steam back on to course to north. We quickly lost sight of it in the fog, but it was something I shall never forget.

It may sound odd, but the biggest bergs are not necessarily the most dangerous. Many small icebergs of all shapes and sizes are seen; very small lumps of ice are known as 'growlers' and are probably the most dangerous sorts of ice for ships to meet at night or in fog, for very little can be seen above water and they can cause fatal damage to a ship if struck at any speed.

The other sort of ice which is such a feature of the Antarctic is, of course, pack ice, and with the possible exception of parts of the Graham Land Peninsula, the whole of the continent is surrounded by a wide expanse of pack ice for much of the year. Even in the 1930's, when I was down there, parts of the coastline had not been sighted and so the Admiralty's South Polar Chart of 1930 was a complete blank in parts. The probable position of the coastline was only indicated by a very irregular pecked line which was explained as "Approximately the furthest South reached hitherto (1930) by any vessel". These cruises were truly voyages of discovery and were very exciting, but also needed a great deal of care and skill in navigation, constantly changing course to negotiate the ice, which of course would extend and recede according to the seasons, so it was never the same. I remember, on one commission, we encountered the edge of the pack ice running west-north-west and so had to alter course, without sighting land. Yet, we were in a similar longitude in February 1936, just 13½ months later, on the following commission, when we found the coast in this region completely clear of pack ice, and we were able to explore a small bay on the coast of Kemp Land, which had not been previously discovered.

That February of 1936 was to be full of surprises for us. We were steaming further south and east than we had done on the previous commission when we had to turn back because of the ice and made good speed, in search of whales for marking, but on the night of the 21st February we found ourselves in a strong westerly gale and so we proceeded south into the Mackenzie Sea to seek shelter during the dark hours. In the morning, the weather was fine and clear, and we proceeded east, expecting to sight Princess Elizabeth Land, which according to our chart formed the east coast of the Mackenzie Sea. We steamed on and on, eastwards, until noon, when we took a sighting and found that, we were in a position which, on the chart, showed us to be ten miles inland!

This was of course a tremendous experience for seafarers, but was not helping us in our main purpose to mark whales, and, as we had not seen any in this region, we turned back westward, steering nor'west, until we rounded Cape Darnby and were clear of the Mackenzie Sea. As we proceeded west, we reached the Scullin Monolith, an extraordinary, rocky peak right on the coast. We steamed into the shallow bay at its foot, and lowered a lifeboat in which a number of us landed on the rocky shore. There was a large penguin rookery here, with hundreds of penguins nesting. It was on this monolith that the Union Jack was raised and a proclamation read on the 13th February 1931. Perhaps more importantly for me, it was the first time that I had set foot on the

Antarctic Continent, although this was my fifth commission to the Antarctic!

All this, of course, took place very nearly sixty years ago, a lifetime for many. In those sixty years, there has been a tremendous increase in our knowledge of the Antarctic, mainly due, it must be said, to the large-scale use of aircraft. What has not changed is the fact that the Antarctic is still surrounded by that wide belt of pack ice which is at its maximum extent in August and September, and its least in February and March. The ice in all its forms is something which Man is not likely to change very much, but Man can do something to protect those whales that have won my respect for a lifetime, and prevent them from becoming extinct.

The irony of truly great men is that their modesty hides their achievements like a miser hides his gold. When asked about his war service, Ron would laugh away the topic with the comment, "I managed to get through the whole war without getting my feet wet." How much more there is to tell, though. He went to war as an officer in the Royal Naval Reserve and was to earn a legendary reputation in anti-submarine warfare, commanding convoy escorts in the North Atlantic in the campaign which lasted from the first days of the war to the last. It was a war which would destroy so much that was valuable, valuable men, valuable ships, valuable hopes. Ron's old company, Blue Star, would suffer as badly as any.

Twenty six days after the outbreak of war the *Arandora Star* arrived at Falmouth to await the Government's decision on how to use her. Eventually it was decided that she had too much top hamper for use as an armed merchant cruiser, so the alternative was to use her as a personnel transport. Experiments were being made at that time to devise a way of intercepting torpedoes and one method was fitted to the *Arandora Star*, a light but strong wire net, slung from the bows and rigged out around the hull.

She went into trooping service and in June 1940 went to Narvik where she had visited in more peaceful times. Then, on the 2nd July 1940 at 0400 hrs she sailed from Liverpool with 174 officers and crew taking German and Italian internees and prisoners of war to Canada. Two and a quarter hours later a torpedo struck and exploded starboard at about the position of the engine room.

The finest cruise ship in the world was lost with the captain and twelve other officers and 42 crew, together with heavy loss of life among the prisoners aboard. For Ron, it was bitter, dispiriting news. Ironic, perhaps, that his war service would play such a part in protecting the merchant shipping upon which he had set out on his career and upon which the survival of his country depended. It was now that Ron Freaker would so truly distinguish himself. He was, indeed, small in stature – he had to stand on a biscuit tin in order to look out over the bridge rail – but in every other way he was a giant.

Ron was in command of a state-of-the-art 'Flower' Class corvette, designed with the latest technology for hunting and destroying submarines, when she docked in the United States. A news-hungry reporter collared him and pressed him for news about this top-secret ship. In the true traditions of the Navy, Ron told him:

"The ship's cat is pregnant."

In the early morning light of the 27th June 1941, Ron was in command of the *Nasturtium* escorting an east-bound convoy across the North Atlantic, when a clear Asdic echo of a U-boat was received. The previous three days had seen heavy action driving off enemy submarine attacks, though and they had used up all their depth charges. *Nasturtium* guided her sister escort *Gladiolus* to the spot where the Asdic echo was identified by steaming over the target, indicating the precise location by turning under full helm to leave an aiming mark in her wake. Ron then gave the order to fire by dipping a flag. After four hours the U-boat surfaced, where its crew abandoned ship. For Ron, it meant a DSO.

In April 1943, Ron commanded the 'River' Class frigate *Jed* in the 1st Escort Group during a battle which was fought for nine days over a thousand square miles of sea and by its close 40 enemy submarines had been in contact, of which six were destroyed and two more lost in collision. In the following month, the Germans lost 43 U-boats all-told, which shocked the High Command and forced the temporary withdrawal of all U-boats from the North Atlantic.

From now on, the tide of the Battle of the Atlantic began to swing for the Allies – and Ron was working just as hard as ever. On the 14th June *Jed* and the sloop *Pelican* were escorting a convoy when a U-boat transmission was detected twenty miles ahead. The U-boat went deep, but the ships attacked with depth charges and the submarine was destroyed. Ron was now awarded a bar to his DSO.

In August, *Jed* took part in an anti- U-boat campaign in the Bay of Biscay, when he was awarded the DSC. There was no let-up, though, and in 1942, commanding the frigate *Loch Eck*, Ron had the benefit of brand new developments in waging anti-submarine warfare. Ultra Intelligence gave advance, accurate information about U-boat sailings from Norway and, in consort with three other frigates, They succeeded in sinking three U-boats with Squid and Hedgehog weapons. Ron was awarded a bar to his DSC.

This war record was almost unsurpassed; in addition to his Polar Medal, Ron had been awarded the DSO and Bar and DSC and Bar. Whatever would he find to do in peacetime?

For much of the nineteenth century, European shipping links with India and the Far East had the enormous obstacle of sailing around the Cape, or, in the case of P & O's service, trekking overland between oceans. Then in 1869, the vision of Frenchman Ferdinand de Lesseps came to fruition with the opening of the Suez Canal, perhaps the most important single factor in the development of nineteenth century maritime trade, clipping weeks off passages to the Far East and Britain's most valuable imperial possessions. It was not only the UK which benefitted, but the entire maritime world, and in a short time the Canal proved itself to be indispensable, an asset which was destined to become more valuable every year. Just how vital an asset it is to world trade can be seen only too clearly by the part which it has played in the arena of armed conflict this century.

Ron was now to join the Suez Canal Pilotage Service. Bearing in mind the importance of the Canal, it was a position of considerable merit, and Ron threw himself into the job with all his enthusiasm. He enjoyed the work enormously, and rose to become Senior Pilot, as the ships which passed through his control steadily grew in the 'fifties into monster crude carriers, the forerunners of the supertankers upon whose fortunes the world's prosperity would depend.

Ron was forced to leave the Suez Canal service in 1956, when Egypt's President Nasser decided that he had had enough of British influence once and for all and prompted a crisis that led to considerable British and French embarrassment, but without a job it was all not much good to Ron and so he returned to the UK. It was not long before he was under way in a new career, though, for, with his elite distinction of having an Extra-Master's Certificate, he joined the Board of Trade as a surveyor and examiner in Southampton. Indeed, half of the present day surveyors and examiners remember Ron taking them for their orals – a harrowing, unforgettable experience, for Ron extended his very high standards to everything he did, and certainly many a candidate quaked in his boots before him! It must always be said in the same breath, though, that they all knew he would be scrupulously fair. As a surveyor, he was just as strict: when ships in port were due for inspection, Ron would cast a very strict eye on them, and nobody, no matter how exalted would escape. Ron's particular duties covered the vital matter of lifeboat inspection, and there is one story of when the Cunarder *Queen Mary* arrived in port, Ron inspected her lifeboats and found some rot in the timbers. He said that they must be replaced, and received the consequent assurances that they would be. On her next arrival back in Southampton, he inspected her and found that the lifeboats had not been repaired. He calmly asked for the ship's Passenger Certificate, with no further explanation, and it was dutifully produced. He then took it, put it in his pocket, and said, "Now you cannot sail until the lifeboats have been repaired." Consternation swept through the mighty Cunard company, but the lifeboats were repaired and the ship sailed.

Ron stayed on for many years after retirement age, and when he did finally retire, he was invited down to the Nautical College at Warsash for a dinner in his honour, an event which was virtually unprecedented and a very strong mark of the respect in which the professional martime community held this man who was noted throughout his life for his extremely strict professional standards and at the same time his enormous sense of humour.

It was not to be the end of his work, though, for, even in his retirement, he coached candidates for their yacht master's certificates near his home at New Milton.

Ron died just before Christmas 1991. As the preacher, a personal friend of his, said at his funeral, "In stature he was very small, but in every other way he was the tallest man I have ever known."

The Wake of the Cachalots

A TRIBUTE TO COMMODORE MACLEAN

*Quotations are taken from the late Commodore MacLean's autobiography 'Queen's Company', for which Donald generously was keen to give his consent.

Donald MacLean grew up in the unforgiving climate of Stornoway, where English was a foreign language, but one which he would have to learn if he was to join the Merchant Service. His father was a boatbuilder and his grandfather had been a square-rigged shipmaster. His own first experience of the sea came in a small, sailing fishing boat, before joining the Cunard Line as apprentice in 1917.

Donald's first ship was a very unglamorous Mediterranean trader of some 1,800 tons, the *Tyria*. They were hard times, in the midst of the First World War, with no end in sight, as the little ship carried ammunition in dangerous convoys, where Morse Code was an important skill, and Donald was quick to learn, which gave him a highly useful advantage.

The war had brought Second and Third officers out of retirement in order to fill the ranks of merchant navy officers, which had been severely depleted. Many were sailing ship era men who hated all the coal smoke and bustle of the modern steamers. Donald remembered his own fellow-apprentice in his book, 'Queen's Company':

"He was an outstandingly fine young man and we got on well together despite the fact that any argument we might have was liable to be settled by a friendly beating with the gloves on. He was too good a fighter for me! I regret to recall that after leaving *Tyria* on the following voyage he was drowned when his new ship, the *Dwinsk*, was torpedoed in a gale in mid-Atlantic. He was barely seventeen at the time."

Within a few years, Donald had worked his way up in the Cunard fleet and in 1925 he was appointed Third Officer of the graceful turbine steamer *Caronia* (20,000 tons), his first 'Atlantic Greyhound'. The sudden luxury was unbelievable to Donald; he explored every corner of the ship, "From the lofty navigating bridge, with its shining array of equipment new to me, down to the elegant public rooms suggestive of Edwardian opulence. In the nature of things one eventually got used to it all, but at first the sheer size of everything seemed overwhelming after the cramped little freighter in which I had been serving."

This was Donald's first experience in the heavy responsibility of ferrying several hundred passengers across the North Atlantic every ten days, not only safely but also happily. After leave of training in the Royal Naval Reserve he joined Cunard's flagship *Aquitania* (45,600 tons), where he dined amid the bejewelled luxury of the Atlantic Ferry, with the rich and famous from prime ministers to movie stars.

In 1934 he joined the great *Mauretania* as Second Officer, his first promotion in nine years. She left Southampton in a snowstorm just before Christmas, bound for New York, which was to be her base for a series of sunshine cruises to the Caribbean.

"The old *Mauretania* had an atmosphere all her own. For one thing, she was positively a ship rather than a floating hotel. She attracted her own special clientele, people who liked movement and the dash of what might almost be called a speed-boat type of travel. For, although a veteran by this time, she was a very frisky one. She might be twenty eight and her décor definitely Victorian, but she had a tremendous turn of speed for her day. Her public rooms were small, her passenger alleyways were narrow, and her decks leaked badly in wet weather. Yet she could cover the whole range of West Indian ports easily on a fortnight's cruise."

On the 26th September 1934, she made her last crossing from New York, averaging nearly 24½ knots. She berthed at Southampton just one month short of 27 years service. On the North Atlantic alone, engaged on her peaceful business, she had covered well over two million miles. While she lay tied up in Southampton, next to her old White Star rival *Olympic*, both awaiting their fate amid the Depression, the *Mauretania* was sold to be broken up at Rosyth.

RMS *Mauretania* sailed on the 1st July 1935. Among the crowd of thousands who turned up to bid farewell, was Sir Arthur Rostron, then Staff Captain of the Southampton Master Mariners' Club. The heroic captain of the *Carpathia* which raced 58 miles to the aid of the *Titanic* in 1912, Rostron had been master of the *Mauretania* for nine years, during when not once did she ever fail him.

The journey to the breakers was full of sentiment, such as, when the place of her berth was slipping astern, she signalled, "Goodbye Tyneside. This is my last radio. Closing down for ever, Mauretania." On this last passage, she was ordered to proceed at 15 knots but she would keep working up to 18. Her engines still were in magnificent condition, greatly due to the loving care bestowed upon her by her engineers, who, like the rest of her ship's company, felt something go out of their lives with her disposal. Perhaps the last word should go to a small, outward-bound tramp steamer who, as she passed the *Mauretania* steaming on her way up to the Forth, hailed her:

"Goodbye Old Lady. It's a damn shame."

Donald's experience in cruising became almost legendary for the ships that he commanded in 'blue waters'. In the 1950's he was given command of the *Britannic* (29,000 tons), the last of the old White Star liners. While the Cunarders like the *Aquitania* and *Mauretania* were narrow and 'lively sea-boats', *Britannic* was much broader in the beam and had no speed to her – but she was the most comfortable of ships in heavy weather and had a devoted passenger list that cruised in her every winter.

"Mink and Diamond Cruising" was how Donald described his voyaging in the *Caronia*, the magnificent 'Green Goddess', one of the happiest ships he served in.

The romance of the Spanish Main was conjured up as the *Caronia* visited places like Port Royal, home of Captain Henry Morgan, the notorious 17th century buccaneer who later became first governor of Jamaica. A century later, Port Royal became the headquarters of the British West Indies Fleet and Lieutenant Horatio Nelson was based here for two years. At Cape Town some of the passengers would leave to go on safari to places as far away as the Belgian Congo and Lake Victoria, rejoining at Mombasa and Zanzibar.

Her passengers were truly fitting to the luxury of mink and diamond cruising. Mrs Horace Dodge, widow of the Detroit motor magnate, loved to give dinner dances, which were splendid affairs where the ladies wore long dresses with white mink stoles and everybody displayed courtly manners. Donald recalled that she was a wonderful octogenarian very young at heart:

"Born in Dundee, Mrs Dodge wasted little time on anyone who presumed on her open nature. I recall at one of the parties in my cabin one evening a brash and recent acquaintance of hers coming over to her and saying, "Tell us about your famous pearls, Anna." Mrs D fixed him with a frosty look and the young man was wise enough to drop the matter instantly. The beads referred to, a double row of gorgeously lustrous pearls which she was then wearing, were reputed to have once belonged to Catherine The Great of Russia."

Cruising in the *Caronia*, they made landfalls from the Roman luxury of Capri to the colonial splendour of Bermuda and the West Indies, through junks in Hong Kong to the bustling harbour

A Tribute to Commodore MacLean

of Rio de Janeiro. In Triston, Donald bought a postage stamp, marked '2d or 8 potatoes'! He paid 2d.

Expense was a secondary consideration for the passengers. Virtually every night some passenger booked the *Caronia's* beautiful Verandah restaurant for a private party and they would have it decorated in the manner to suit the part of the world where they were presently visiting, and guests would have to dress in appropriate costume.

What greater contrasts could possibly be imagined in anybody's life, than these scenes of carefree happiness compared with Donald's dreadful experiences in the Second World War. Donald joined the *Transylvania* (17,000 tons) ten days after war broke out. The flagship of the old Anchor Line, which Cunard had bought out in November 1911, had been taken out of service and fitted out as an armed merchant cruiser, but within three weeks she was ready and a commissioning party was held in her beautifully panelled smokeroom.

"Among our guests that evening was the ship's former master, Captain Bone and his wife. David Bone, a brilliant raconteur, regailed us with stories of his early days at sea in the famous China tea-clippers. He lunched on board several times and never failed to delight us with his stories. They owed much to his gift of mimicry. All his characters, Welsh, French or Chinese, established themselves in a moment. In their middle years David Bone and Joseph Conrad had been close friends...."

They sailed for Scapa Flow in the Orkneys, where they arrived on the 12th October, seeing the great names like HMS *Royal Oak* aswell as those ships that would shortly win immortality for their bravery, P & O's *Rawalpindi* and Shaw Savill's *Jervis Bay*. Two days later the *Royal Oak* was sunk.

At first light the *Transylvania* and *Rawalpindi* were ordered to proceed immediately to patrol off Iceland. The two ships accompanied each other for twelve hours before parting in a blinding hail-squall off Cape Wrath. Donald recalled:

"On November 23rd I had just returned from boarding a Norwegian tanker. It was a miserable day with rain and sleet squalls but in *Transylvania's* ward room it was cosy as I sat down to a mug of tea and a smoke. Presently 'Bunts' (the signalman) entered and placed a signal pad on the table between the first lieutenant and myself. It was from *Rawalpindi* and in 'self-evident' code. It read "Enemy battleships in sight.'"

The brave *Rawalpindi* hardly had time to send that signal when she was bombarded by the eleven inch guns of the *Scharnhorst* and *Gneisenau*. Ordering the *Rawalpindi's* eight 6 inch guns to return fire, Captain E C Kennedy put up a magnificent fight. His ship lasted another sixteen minutes but the story of her stubborn fight to the end rallied the spirit of the British People when it was at its lowest ebb.

Donald MacLean's own destiny met him, when, "During one of our lay-overs on the Clyde, in February 1940, I was exercising the boarding cutter's crew when an enormous grey-painted ship descended the river and anchored close to us. In letters thirty inches high on the bow was painted the name 'Queen Elizabeth.' In a moment of professional exuberance I listened to the pleadings of two of my midshipmen – and boarded the colossus. It was perhaps our most pleasant boarding job of the war."

U-Boat torpedoes had easy targets in the tall superstructures of great liners and before they could be replaced by more suitable naval cruisers, twelve of these fine passeneger vessels were lost, with heavy loss of life and grossing nearly a quarter of a million tons between them. On the 8th August 1940, *Transylvania* sailed from Belfast with a new battery of eight 6 inch guns, gun shields and a counter-mine degaussing girdle.

On the stroke of midnight there was a dreadful shudder and the ship seemed to be heeling over to starboard as alarm bells rang shrilly throughout the ship.

"The torpedo had torn an enormous gash in the port side amidships, and despite the valiant efforts of the damage control party the main machinery space was soon awash. Shortly afterwards the bulkhead collapsed under the pressure and the cold Atlantic cascaded into the after-holds. So great was the pressure that the after-hold covers were blown off.

"Working in pitch-blackness we tried to close the hatch-covers but the ship appeared doomed. The order 'Abandon Ship' was given but the stricken vessel, yawing helplessly in her toils, had swung head to wind and with davits aslant this made it extremely difficult to lower the lifeboats. I got all the lifeboats possible away from the after deck while Commander Shaw saw to the forward section. I rushed to the bridge, now tilted steeply skywards, advising Captain Miles that our stern was quickly disappearing under water. Grasping the sloping bridge rails and unruffled as ever, Miles was anxiously watching the starboard boats pulling clear of the ship.

""Ensure that everyone is off the after end, and get away as quickly as possible. I don't think we will remain afloat much longer."

"When I returned to the after deck there was nobody left save Bradley and an assistant paymaster. We clambered over the high side and slid down the ship's bottom, dropping into an overcrowded lifeboat. So great was the pressure in the boat that several ratings slipped over the gunwale and swam alongside. I had been in the boat for about ten uneasy minutes when a heavy swell capsized her and those of us who survived swam away to whatever floated. Very soon everyone was covered in fuel oil and before long men could be heard moaning and gasping in the darkness. One young swimmer, already tossed out of one lifeboat and apparently exhausted, clutched me tightly round the neck and with difficulty I persuaded him to swim towards the mast and gear which had floated away from the capsized boat. It took me some time to realize that the youngster's vision had been impaired by searing oil fuel.

"As the night wore on the numbing cold and the constant effort to avoid drowning when big seas swept clean over us were beginning to blunt the will to hang on. About 5 am, when hope was perhaps at its lowest, a dark shape loomed up and passed close by us. Several men in the water yelled out and shortly afterwards a blue light mercifully probed in our direction. A flotanet was flung out in our direction and we swam feebly over the top of it. As soon as there were sufficient men in the net it was snatched inboard and we were dumped unceremoniously on to the destroyer's deck like a catch of herrings. A seaman bent me double across a wooden bench whereupon I vomited violently, after which I was taken below and placed in a hammock on the seamen's mess deck. Someone in a white boiler suit rinsed my eyes, nostrils and mouth with a soothing alkaline wash."

Twenty years later the editor of the 'Dundee Sunday Post' sent Donald a copy of a letter written to the newspaper by the sister of that youngster who had clung to Donald in the water. The lady wrote saying that she had read of Donald's retirement and wanted him to know that his heartening words had saved her brother's life.

More was to be in store for Donald's war, when, in command of the frigate *Cygnet*, he witnessed the terrible hardships of the Arctic Convoys to Russia, and saw the dogged determination of an irrepressible People to survive. When he left *Cygnet* for the Mediterranean Fleet in September 1944, he truly felt a lump in his throat. "We had been through many an unrecorded tough spot together."

When Donald eventaully returned home at the end of the war, he opened a letter appointing him Chief Officer of the *Aquitania*, and once again the elegance of the Cunarders awaited him. Cruising was grand, but his strongest feelings followed the hoisting of his Commodore's Burgee in *Queen Elizabeth* on the 19th May 1960. Donald's reminiscences of command in this mightiest of liners are recounted fully in his book and the Cunard 'Queens' are undoubtedly the most widely-documented ships in maritime history, but perhaps we should just end with Donald's account of the final stage of his last voyage, from 'Queen's Company':

"By evening we were passing through that haven of happy yachtsmen, Cowes Roads; and as the tugboats eased us into our berth in the Ocean Terminal in Southampton the last rays of a lovely sunset lingered over the New Forest, and as I looked aft the quartermaster was hauling down my burgee. In the wheelhouse the navigator was collecting his charts. I took one last look round the bridge – everything was shipshape to the end.

""Well, Commodore – here we are back in berth once more – and the end of a long road for you." Jack Holt, our Pilot, was voicing my own thoughts."

A Tribute to Commodore MacLean

Stirring tales of history, that capture the very essence of the Cachalots. And now laid to rest, for Commodore MacLean died in the spring of 1991, within a few days of Jack Holt....

The Wake of the Cachalots

OCEAN EXPRESS: REG KELSO AND THE UNION-CASTLE LINE

By the middle of the nineteenth century, the Peninsular and Oriental Steam Navigation Company's steamships were sailing from Southampton to all the Red on the Atlas, the Mediterranean, Egypt, India and the Far East. They needed huge quantities of good steam coal, but one of the main difficulties at the time was obtaining this coal, because it was transported almost entirely by sea around the coast, which was an extremely expensive operation, but the only way possible. Founder and chairman, Arthur Anderson, was one of the greatest names in shipping history, who in P and O had forged the greatest company trading to the colonies; Anderson clearly had a big incentive to resolve the problem with the supply of coal and so in 1853 he founded a company to bring coal to Southampton by steam collier. But when, in 1854, Britain went to war with the Russians in the Crimea, P and O vessels were chartered to the Government as troopships and Anderson's new Union Company ships were employed on the routes temporarily vacated by the P and O ships. The Union Line prospered on the routes until 1856, when war ended and the P and O ships returned home. While the directors were wondering where to find a new job, in the summer of 1857 the Admiralty invited tenders for a mail service to South Africa and the Union Line promptly won the contract. This contract required a voyage time of 42 days on a monthly service and when the company's *Dane* sailed from Southampton in September 1857 at short notice she carried only six passengers, but from this beginning grew the service that continued for nearly 120 years and gave employment to hundreds of seafarers.

The Wake of the Cachalots

High Summer of imperial travel; pilot aboard, the Athlone Castle dwarfs a "monster" flying boat as she sails for the cape

The Union Line had settled down well in the South African trade by 1862, when a tough Scots businessman from the Clyde, Donald Currie, formed his own shipping company to operate sailing ships on the India run to Calcutta. Rather than buy second-hand tonnage, he had his own ships built: constructed of iron, they grossed on average 1,200 tons and were named after British castles. With his competitive drive, Currie made a successful name for himself and in 1868 the *Tantallon Castle* broke the Calcutta record.

As the diamond-propsecting industry developed in South Africa, the necessary machinery, railway equipment and other imports poured into the country. Indeed, the diamond yield proved so impressive that it made more profit than all the country's agricultural revenues combined. Currie was beginning to take notice. The Cape and Natal Line had been formed on the strength of the diamond boom but was failing to compete with the Union Line and while Currie was chartering two ships to the Cape Line, it collapsed, and he was then persuaded to continue the service to the Cape himself. The service was restructured with new steamers and when the brand new *Walmer Castle* arrived in cape Town on the 4th October, 1872, having taken just 24 days from London, the Union Line found itself with a competitor. These two companies would now leave all other rivals standing in their own incredible rivalry for supremacy on the Cape Run.

As the Castle Line built up its fleet with more powerful steamships, the Union Line responded magnificently with their own newbuildings. Both companies saw their supremacy as vital and dared not allow their rival to get ahead of them. It led to an incredible race to build a better fleet, producing larger ships which carried more passengers in a shorter voyage-time in fast-improving accommodation, all at alarming expense. In 1880 the Castle Line introduced the first ships on the route to reach 3,000 tons, which the Union Line promptly had to surpass: they did, with the *Trojan*, grossing 3,650 tons and the amazing luxury of electric lighting in the saloon! Still the South African trade boomed, forcing Currie to rival the *Trojan* with the graceful *Garth Castle* and *Drummond Castle*. Unflinchingly, the Union Line determined to race in front again and in 1882 they introduced the *Athenian* and *Moor*.

Then suddenly trade fell sharply, forcing many ships onto other routes or to be laid up. After the huge capital investment in recent years, the slump was giving really serious headaches to both companies. Then in 1886 gold was discovered on the Rand and overnight the emigrant trade to South Africa grew heavier than ever. The demand for passages was so high that on Castle Line ships emigrants were ordered to "sleep where any place can be found by the Chief Steward".

In 1890 Currie put into service by far the largest ship on the route to date. The *Dunottar Castle* grossed 5,625 tons, with accommodation for 360 passengers which could be increased by a further 150 in "open berth" accommodation. On her maiden voyage she broke the Cape record by completing the voyage in 17 days 20 hours. The homeward voyage was even faster: she docked in 16 days 14 hours.

This momentarily sent the Union Line reeling. They soon recovered, though and in December 1890 launched the *Scot*, 6,884 tons, with twin screws and accommodation for 408 passengers. She sailed on her maiden voyage on the 25th July 1891 and broke the record by docking in Cape Town in 14 days 9 hours 52 minutes, including a stop at Madeira. In 1893, she arrived at Cape Town two days before her expected time, having made the voyage in 14 days 18 hours 57 minutes, a record that would stand for more than forty years.

Currie had to make a new plan to beat the Union Line again. This rivalry was causing problems for both companies, though, for their intense rivalry was crippling the balance sheets. When the Boer War broke out in 1899, the two operators were ideal to provide the ships to transport the 450,000 troops needed there, and they were paid for these trooping duties, but what they needed was peace-time trade figures.

In order to ensure the keenest service, for years the Cape Government had included in successive mail contracts a clause forbidding them to amalgamate. A new contract was due in 1900 and this time the Government announced that the contract would be awarded to one company only and invited tenders. Over the years the Union Line and the Castle Line had found an unshakeable respect for one another, though, which somehow

Captain Kelso in command

outshone their financial troubles. Both companies failed to submit tenders – they declined to force the other into extinction. Once again, therefore, the Cape Government divided the contract between them, but this time there was no clause barring amalgamation. Sir Donald Currie was a man of vision and swiftly saw his big opportunity. In December 1899 it was made public that the two boards had agreed on terms whereby the Union Steamship Company was absorbed by the Castle Mail Packet Company and on the 8th March 1900 the Union-Castle Mail Steamship Company Limited came into being.

Without that cut-throat rivalry, schedules were fixed and kept, so that more efficient arrangements could be made for passenger journeys and cargo deliveries and fixed 'mail days' became established. Moreover, no longer did they have to face huge coaling bills from very fast passages which were a boost for prestige but were bad for the balance sheet.

This was the foundation of the Union-Castle Line, an operation that was responsible for the careers and the livelihoods of so many sons of Southampton, home of its express passenger mailship fleet, where the adage "Every Thursday at Four O'Clock" became a by-word, for you could set your clock by a Union-Castle liner's departure. It is the story, also, of a great many master mariners, who hailed from many parts of the Kingdom. Like Captain Reg Kelso. His story starts on the cadet training schoolship 'Conway':

From time to time life on the schoolship 'Conway' was enlivened by the return of former cadets splendidly attired in uniform and pockets ajingle with money. Having paid their respects to the hierarchy they then descended to the mess decks to meet with their former cronies and others fortunate enough to be permitted to listen to their stories of life at sea.

Royal Naval midshipmen had invariably retained their metal cap-stretchers and their perfectly formed caps were in marked contrast to those of their Merchant Navy colleagues whose battered and mis-shapen caps had been lovingly formed to reflect their 'old salt' image.

The war was just drawing to a close and some of their stories were sad ones, bringing news of the death of some who were only names to many of us by virtue of their prowess on the rugby field or in the boxing ring but invariably the casual mention of foreign ports sent a tingle down my spine. They tripped off their tongues without thought or effort and for a brief second each one conjured up its own picture in the listener's mind.

Then there were the cap badges. The well shaped caps sported the Royal Navy badge but the headwear of the Merchantmen sported a vast variety, each one depicting the chosen shipping company of the wearer. Of these the most distinctive was the Blue Star Line and the least was Alfred Holt. In between lay the designs of the Peninsular and Oriental, Shaw Savill, Palm Line, Clan Line, Pacific Steam Navigation Company, the list was endless.

I can never recall a Union-Castle cadet returning to 'Conway' but my interest in the company was aroused during my early morning arrivals in Belfast by steamer when proceeding home on leave. At that time the Union-Castle ships with their distinctive lavender grey hulls and red and black funnels were being refitted at Harland and Wolff where they had been built and as the steamer navigated the Pollock Channel I invariably saw the squat outline of one of them.

I applied to join the company in January 1946 (I was due to leave 'Conway' in April) and got a brusque reply. I could, if I wished, apply nearer to my completion date and if there were any vacancies I would be granted an interview. I discussed the situation with my shipmates and we agreed that it might be better to try elsewhere. I wrote to Alfred Holt and to Blue Star, and both agreed to give me an interview at a later date.

The weeks passed until, in early March, I received a letter from Union-Castle instructing me to report for interview in Glasgow two days hence. I was duly despatched and returned to 'Conway' two days later with a promise of immediate employment as a cadet with The Union-Castle Mail Steamship Company. Final examinations were long-forgotten as I packed my bags and after the customary farewell party for a few chosen friends at the County Hotel, Bangor, I returned home for a short leave and kitting out.

On the 2nd April I joined the night steamer in Belfast and arrived in Glasgow next morning where, in accordance with my instructions, I joined *Good Hope Castle* at Number 2 Ballasting Crane, Queens Dock. As I reached the top of the gangway a young man in a white jacket appeared from a doorway and said the never-to-be-forgotten phrase, "Good morning, Sir, have you had breakfast?"

Immediately I was aware of a feeling of welcome, of warmth and of friendship – feelings which never left me, afloat or ashore, during the next forty two years. Years which were to see the decline of those great fleets whose former servants had held us spellbound on our 'Conway' seachests, splendid in their liveries and steadfast in their loyalties. Years which saw the decline and fall of the Union-Castle Line and the disappearance of the 'Castle' name from the oceans of the world. Years which were very different from those we had grown to expect but which, in their own way, were every bit as exciting and rewarding.

Life in Union-Castle centred around the Southampton-based mailship fleet. At table on the cargo ships much of the conversation was of earlier service in the mailships and those of us yet to enjoy those delights listened spellbound to lusty stories of romance and abandon under the tropic moon. Sometimes loading newsprint in the snowy wastes of Cornerbrook or sugar in the steaming cauldron of Port Louis, our thoughts strayed to the delights to come and spirits were rekindled.

My first mailship was *Capetown Castle* and I joined her with a brand new Second Mate's Certificate. This in itself was an innovation because hitherto Junior Fourth Officers were all holders of a First Mate's Certifcate, at least, and most had Master's but in this post-war period more tonnage was being manned and such luxuries had to be trimmed.

As Junior Officer of the Watch one had a well-established routine and woe betide the upstart who tried to exceed his authority. After 'steadying on' the steering compass and the standard compass and checking the compass error by celestial bearing, one retired to the wing of the bridge unless invited into the wheelhouse by the Senior – a very unlikely event. Talking to the Bridge Quartermaster or Bridge Boy was frowned upon, unless absolutely necessary, and although many of those reporting to the bridge could impart their messages to you, they nevertheless had to be directed to the wheelhouse where the Senior Watchkeeper, seated on the flag locker, talked horses with the Steering Quartermaster. Rounds of the exterior passenger decks had to be completed quickly and discreetly with anything of a contentious nature avoided lest the Senior Officer be called upon to write a report. A change of Steering Quartermaster dictated another 'steadying on' and another compass error check, then back to the bridge wing again until it was time to call the next watch.

By day, passengers had to be shown around the bridge and during this time the Senior invariably stalked the bridge wing mouthing at the Junior "Get rid of them" unless a pretty woman in the party engaged him in conversation. The social life was everything we had heard about it during our cadetship. Meals were taken in the First Class Dining Room complete with orchestra and frock-coated head waiter. One dressed in mess kit with stiff, starched shirt and wing collar and after a week the two paged menu became almost boring and the fillet mignon ceased to be a novelty.

We were not encouraged to mix with the passengers ("Be polite but do not seek to prolong the conversation") but we needed no encouragement and we DID. We were forbidden to entertain in our cabins but were seldom caught and it became an art form to spend every penny of our weekly twenty one shilling bond allowance. Passenger prices were more expensive than ours, so signing cards on deck was a costly exercise and one had to weigh up the possible advantages of doing so.

In port we worked watches and in our off duty periods we enjoyed South African hospitality to the full, playing golf, cricket and rugby, climbing Table Mountain, and supervising the cargo work while awaiting with dread the arrival of the letter promoting us to Third Officer of a cargo ship. The radio room kept us fully informed of the movements of our contemporaries and every chartroom had an updated staff list of each ship in the fleet, which was scoured anxiously to see who might be the next to move.

On arrival at Southampton, every deck officer was interviewed by the Marine Superintendent and not until that was over, could he return to the ship and change into civilian clothes to proceed on leave. Not everybody was granted leave and sometimes one was appointed to staff duties looking after the 'dead' mailship in Southampton pending the return of her sea staff. Officially there was no eating on board at such times and one was paid a subsistence allowance to cover food and 'digs' ashore. Eventually, after one of our number keeled over when tallying mails and was diagnosed as suffering from malnutrition, we were given a lunch meal (and reduced subsistence) but it was still a generous settlement and one could maintain one's social life and still eat enough to keep fit without running into debt.

The Round Africa ships were based in London. For many years the London Office and the Southampton Office had enjoyed a rivalry spawned during the years of the Union Line and the Castle Line . In the Southampton Office an instruction to proceed to London docks to join a ship was given in tones of disapproval – and with a modest degree of sympathy – while anyone arriving in Southampton from a London-based ship was treated with suspicion and a good deal of reserve until they had been in port for some time and had abandoned their slovenly London habits.

It was little different in the London Dock Office. There they pretended that the mailships did not exist and anyone reporting there from Southampton was treated to a diatribe about London standards and how one was here to work. London staff officers lived in rather less luxury than did their Southampton counterparts but the subsistence allowance was equally generous and the fleshpots of West Ham and North Woolwich beckoned.

In those early days one spiralled through promotion always returning to the Mail Fleet to renew acquaintances and then disappearing off into the realms of the cargo ships or London-based passenger ships before being promoted back to the Mails once again. Third Officer Cargo Ship was followed by Third Officer Round Africa, then Second Officer Cargo Ship, Third Officer Mailship, Extra Second Officer Round Africa, Second Officer Mailship, Chief Officer Cargo, First Officer Mail, Chief Officer Round Africa, Chief Officer Mailship; then Command Cargo Ship. That was the laid-down career pattern, although in practice such a well-defined course was seldom followed and temporary promotions or demotions were commonplace.

In 1956 the Union-Castle Line and the Clan Line merged to form The British and Commonwealth Shipping Company and before long the Clan Line officers of all disciplines were serving in passenger vessels and Union-Castle officers were serving in Clan cargo ships. It was a painless exercise, though and many friendships from training ship days were renewed.

The mailships were, in reality, large cargo-carrying ships with luxurious accommodation for some seven hundred passengers and it was this that contributed to their demise. The handling of the large amounts of cargo was labour intensive, time consuming and very, very expensive. New cargo handling methods were being developed in the early 'sixties – containerisation was the 'in' word – and British and Commonwealth was not slow in getting involved with this new technology.

The mail schedule was speeded up in order to allow it to be maintained with a smaller fleet; but the art of passenger carrying had been perfected in the air and long-distance jets with their ever-increasing passenger capacities were making inroads into the monopoly that the Union-Castle Line had enjoyed for years. The effect of all this manifested itself truly in 1963 when the company announced that tenders were being invited for the construction of two fast cargo liners, with no passenger accommodation because it was felt that berths offered in the five passenger ships in service were adequate to meet the demand. Thus the *Southampton Castle* and *Good Hope Castle* were the first mailships ever built without passenger accommodation.

It had always been my ambition to command a mailship and now it began to look as if that dream was to be thwarted. On top of the changes that I have outlined, the merger of Union-Castle and Clan Line had resulted in not only a vastly increased fleet but also an equally vastly increased officer list, in an era when company salaries were seen as in need of pruning, which all had the effect of slowing down promotion. My career followed the more or less traditional path until 1964, when a new rank, of Staff Commander, was introduced into the Mail Fleet. It was really an upgrading of the Chief Officer's position but was rather more lucrative and much more prestigious. In London I was summoned to the Dock Office and told, with some disdain, that I was being relieved as Chief Officer of the Round Africa *Kenya Castle* and was to proceed to Southampton for an appointment as Staff Commander of the mailship *Pendennis Castle*.

The merger certainly widened our professional horizons and instead of the spiralling promotion path we had come to expect we now found ourselves called up to serve in a much wider variety of ships. The British and Commonwealth group included the King Line, Scottish Tankers, Bowater Steamship Company and several other operators and we, as loyal British and Commonwealth men were expected to serve in any of them. Bowaters ran a fleet of small paper carrying ships trading to the South American continent and to Scandinavia and these ships became popular for 'first command' appointments.

In 1967 I was appointed to command, and leaving the luxury of the mailship *Edinburgh Castle* and the cushy life of Staff Commander, I proceeded to Northfleet, a Thames riverside berth, to take command of the *Gladys Bowater*, 5,475 deadweight tons. After *Edinburgh Castle*'s 28,705 gross tons she seemed very small indeed but it was amazing how big she suddenly became when I was first called upon to handle her. With Company Pilot in attendance we sailed down river to the Swale and the port of Ridham. Entering the narrow waterway and the tortuous approaches to Ridham Dock, the pilot pointed out to me the various damages inflicted by previous ships, commanded, I was sure, by ex-Staff Commanders.

We sailed out into the teeth of a gale and as we cleared Dungeness I very soon realised that there was a vast difference between little ships in bad weather and big ships in bad weather. She stood on end, rolled alarmingly and every endeavour to improve things by reducing speed or altering course had little effect. The crew, realising that they were in the hands of yet another mailship escapee, were totally nonplussed and pretended that it was not really happening. In fact they were mostly Bowater men and knew little better weather. We berthed in Charlestown, South Carolina, after almost being run down by an American nuclear submarine on trials, but by that time I had come to terms

The Gladys Bowater, *Reg's first command*

The Reina del Mar *on idyllic cruising*

with my new job. They were excellent sea ships and well equipped with navigational aids and cargo handling gear.

Some seven months later, just as I was preparing to sail from the Manchester Ship Canal, I was relieved and ordered to report to Southampton as Assistant Marine Superintendent on a two year posting. We lived in London but a few weeks before I took up my new post I found a suitable house in Bursledon, near Southampton, and my wife and son were soon installed. The mailships came and went and we looked after their requirements, kept them cleaned and painted, met them on arrival to help deal with the problems, exercised the crews in emergency drills in the presence of a Department of Transport surveyor and despatched them to sea in, hopefully, a better condition than when they arrived. We had our own Shore Gang of seamen, riggers and painters and it was now that I was to come into contact with the realities of trade unionism.

The cruise ship *Reina del Mar* was one of our busiest customers and her one-day turnarounds kept us on our toes. She had been built for the Pacific Steam Navigation Company, a British company serving the west coast of South America. The ubiquitous downturn in demand and profitability, though, led to her early demise on the route and she was sold to Union-Castle for cruising.

My two year appointment stretched to almost three and then I joined my first Asian crew ship. The *Clan Maclachlan* was a 6,000 ton general cargo ship and we loaded in Birkenhead for South Africa. By this time fleet reductions were the order of the day and it was no great surprise after a few months to be told to take her to Shanghai for demolition. We left the UK with cargo for South Africa and Hong Kong en route for Shanghai.

Twelve days later, after three typhoons, standing by an American ship aground on a reef, returning to Hong Kong for more fuel and being scrutinised by Chinese Nationalist gunboats, we arrived in Shanghai. We had eleven happy days there handing over the ship to the Chinese crew and, despite the fact that she had been sold for demolition, she left the port under her new name (*East Wind*) but in Clan Line colours for further trading.

After a Tanker Safety Course at Warsash, I was appointed to command the 20,000 ton products tanker *Hector Heron* on charter to British Petroleum. We traded from the Persian Gulf to the River Congo and from there to Australia. We were the last non-Australian flag ship to carry cargo around the Australian Coast and fortuitously were in the right place at the right time to rescue three young men from a capsized trimaran in wretched conditions off Australia's east coast. I was relieved in Lagos and came home to join the bulk carrier *King James* on charter to British Steel. We traded to West Africa, New Orleans, Narvik and the Continent, becoming the largest ship at that time to navigate the Ghent – Terneuzen Canal, and certainly one of the few to navigate it in reduced visibility which set-in suddenly and without warning.

Just as I was beginning to think that my move to live in Southampton had been rather premature, I was appointed to command the *Reina Del Mar* for a series of cruises from Southampton to the Atlantic Islands and the Mediterranean. It was exciting and very rewarding work to see so many people obviously enjoying themselves. Many passengers returned to the ship year after year and it was a bit shattering for the newly appointed Captain to be told, "You are new, aren't you" and to find that the questioner had done more cruises in the ship than you had. *Reina del Mar* was an old ship and not particularly fuel-efficient and she, too, fell victim to new developments in cruising. Fly-cruises were becoming popular and this, coupled with the fact that she was labour-intensive soon put her at a disadvantage economically. I commanded her on her last voyage from the United Kingdom and she then went to South Africa to do three or four South American cruises before heading east for demolition.

My next appointment was to the *S A Vaal*, the renamed *Transvaal Castle*, now owned by Safmarine but managed and operated by Union-Castle. She was a magnificent ship and was revolutionary insofar as she was an hotel-class ship with varying standards of accommodation but with all passengers, whether berthed in the best suite or in a four-berth inner, enjoying the same public rooms and other amenities. She was one of the first ships to employ females as stewards in the dining rooms and their influence on the ship was considerable and very advantageous.

She had the most magnificent accommodation for the Captain and from my dayroom I enjoyed a panoramic view of the horizon from beam to beam.

By now, British and Commonwealth were well on the way to achieving their avowed intent to get out of shipping and concentrate on more lucrative business. Ships were being sold at an alarming rate and we knew that the mailships had not much longer to run. I transferred to *Edinburgh Castle*, a ship in which I had served in many capacities during my career. Just twelve hours before we were due to sail, the ship was called upon to host the annual luncheon of the Southampton Master Mariners' Club. The function had been scheduled to be held aboard Shaw Savill's *Southern Cross* but she developed engine trouble returning from a cruise and was drifting in the Channel as the guests boarded *Edinburgh Castle*. The crew enjoyed the challenge and it was an excellent function.

I made three more voyages in the ship, with a break in between for secondment to the London office and it was during this period that I was invited to take up the post of Chief Marine Superintendent for British and Commonwealth. I knew that we would not be shipowning for much longer but was assured that ship management was very much a possibility. I went off to think it over and soon decided that a life at sea in small cargo ships would probably bore me to tears and, in any event, I had my family to think of. I made my last voyage to sea in *Edinburgh Castle* and, in November 1975, I rang "Finished with Engines" on her bridge telegraphs for the last time. I had had twenty nine marvellous years at sea and now a new career was beginning.

Reg certainly considered himself lucky to have the luxury of a new career assured, especially marine-based, if ashore, for the Red Duster was disappearing under the effect of economic attack. By the mid-1970's the British shipping industry was so beset with problems that it did not need any more bad news. Certainly it did not need the embargo on oil supplies inposed by the Arabs following the 1973 Arab-Israeli War, the effect of which was to send the cost of fuel oil soaring. Shipping companies had to consider ways of compromising on the amount of fuel and at the same time increase revenue. The Union-Castle Line slowed down its Cape service by a full day, so reducing its fuel bill, and fares increased sharply. Still, it was not enough: overheads were too high to compete; too many passengers had been lost to air travel and cargoes were being containerised. In 1979 Union-Castle issued the following press release:

"It is with great regret that Union-Castle...announce that the two remaining passenger mailships operating on the route between the United Kingdom and South Africa are to be withdrawn from service in the latter part of 1977..."

This was virtually the end of the old Union-Castle trade but for Reg Kelso, the years after he came ashore were, in their own way, every bit as exciting as had been the 29 years seafaring:

The sale of the ships continued apace, many of my friends were made redundant and eventually we changed from shipowning to ship management. That carried on for a time but we found it almost impossible to compete with the vast number of companies, mostly based in the Far East, who had entered the ship management field. We were, of course, still employing British officers and ratings on UK conditions of service and, in consequence, our costs were high.

Our managed fleet diminished and finally, as we were on the verge of calling it a day and shutting up shop, we were approached by an Italian company and were asked to quote for the management of four refrigerated cargo ships. We quoted on the conventional manning basis and our quote was rejected. We sat around a table and drew up a scheme whereby we would employ our own officers and Bangladeshi ratings. This time we were successful. The officers were paid a flat rate, in US dollars, for six months employment and two months leave and were on a contract of employment with a company registered in Bermuda. We were no longer direct employers of these officers but their loyalty remained and the savings we made enabled us to carry on and afford many of them reasonably gainful employment.

By this time, British and Commonwealth Shipping was a thing of the past and we had changed our name. We were to change it again very soon afterwards when our Italian friends became our employers. The fleet grew and by the end of 1987 we were

The Wake of the Cachalots

managing ten ships with two new ones building in Korea. Much of early 1988 was spent in Korea with the two newbuildings and we ran trials on the first of them in the spring of that year. On the way home I called at Bangladesh to recruit deck and engineering officers – like most companies, we were experiencing difficulty in recruiting British officers – and in May I returned to my desk in London.

The pensionable age had been reduced to sixty and I had attained that age in February 1988. Enjoyable as the life was, it was not what my background had really trained me for and I was finding it more and more difficult to come to terms with crew reductions and the other measures necessary to remain competitive. In August 1988 I made my decision, chose my successor and cleared my desk for the last time. A career of forty two years lay behind me and I remembered each and every one of them with happiness and not a little pride.

"Would I do it all again?" You bet I would, and in exactly the same way. Almost.

RICHARD WHISTLER – THE CACHALOTS SAIL ON

Richard's story gives us a glimpse into the present-day profession of the British Master – and his future. The ship in which Richard Whistler is Master Under God is the descendant of the hard-worked, hungry tramps that plied the world's oceans for whatever cargo could bring them a profit: but these modern vessels are massive, hi-tech ships, chartered on the Baltic Exchange for cargoes of hundreds of thousands of tonnes worth many millions of pounds apiece. They are the bulk carriers.

British bulk shipping is dominated by just a handful of companies, who grasped the potential of the economies of scale by using bigger ships to offer cheaper charter rates to the shipper. By the 1950's the high overheads involved in operating cargo ships was causing many British companies to lose out to competitors from emergent and Far East countries, and they were having to think hard about how to beat the competitors. The answer came in the form of moving cargoes in ever-bigger ships. In 1960, some 230,000,000 tonnes of dry cargo such as iron ore and grain were carried in bulk, six years later the figure was 340,000,000 tonnes. At that time, it cost £750,000 to build a 10,000 deadweight tonne bulk carrier, that is, £75 a tonne. A 23,000 DWT ship cost £50 per tonne to build, though, and a 40,000 tonne ship just £45 per tonne. Moreover, when underway, an 80,000 tonne vessel cost 66% less than a 10,000 tonne ship did, although the percentage reduced dramatically when the ship was in port, not earning money. So, the bigger the vessel, the cheaper it was to carry each tonne of cargo and therefore the cheaper the charter rate could be fixed on the Baltic Exchange, to undercut the competitors and still make a profit. This had been the underlying principle of shipping for centuries – it always will be. The industry was doing what it always had done – it was evolving.

The economies of scale prompted an old and respected company founded by Robert Ropner in the Victorian days of tramping, to build the *Stonepool* in 1966, with the ability to lift 45,027 tonnes of cargo. It was now the dawning of the age of the bulkship company, and soon Ropners had a rival in the shape of another old and highly respected name in Britsh shipping, Furness Withy, a rivalry that was destined to flourish. The British Steel Corporation owned a fleet of large bulk carriers to carry iron ore, coal, whatever was needed for their steel works in the UK. It was Furness Withy whom British Steel appointed to manage their fleet. As was so often the case in shipping, Furness Withy had bought a major interest in another shipping company in 1911, when they negotiated the purchase of a majority shareholding in the respected company of Houlder Brothers. Houlders then made their name operating fast services for passengers and refrigerated cargo services between the UK and South America.

This was the fleet that Richard Whistler found when he joined the company in the '60's, but Furness Withy were restructuring their entire operations, and made Houlder Brothers the bulkship management arm of the group. When the South American Saint Line's *St Essylt, St Thomas* and *St John* were sold in 1965 the company's goodwill and conference rights passed to the ownership of Ore Carriers Limited, itself subsequently owned by British Steel and so the management of all this passed to Furness Withy.

Come the 1980's there was intense rivalry nationwide for the management of British Steel's prestigious bulkships which were confidently expected to remain under the British flag for some time to come, when Richard Whistler was appointed Master of the British Steel Corporation's *Abbey*, 118,750 deadweight tonnes, and then the mighty, state-of-the-art bulk carrier *British Steel* (173,028 DWT). Furness Withy were also awarded the management contract for the new *Ironbridge*, but Ropners secured management of British Steel's two latest newbuildings.

The inevitable overtook this business when in March 1990 British Steel announced its decision to transfer from the UK flag to a 'flag of convenience' in order to reduce its overheads and no doubt to enhance its image in readiness for its privatisation. This of course was nothing new, and indeed as early as 1957, London And Overseas Freighters, pioneers in operating large bulk carriers, had flagged out to an independent register in order to reduce crew costs.

In the same year, 1990, Furness Withy underwent another enormous change when the German company Hamburg-Sudamerikanische Dampschiffarhts-Gesellschaft bought the company from the Tung Group of Hong Kong. It was a sign for the good of the future of European shipping, but one could hardly keep up with such crucial events in the big business of modern shipping. As Omar Khayyam wrote,

> 'The moving finger writes; and having writ, Moves on:'

But, behind all this big business, what of the seafarers who serve these mighty bulkships built at a cost of many millions of pounds and bristling with the most advanced technical navigation and engineering equipment in the world, owned by European-based companies, operated by crews from many nations whom the Master must control, with cargoes still fixed on the Baltic Exchange, as they have for centuries?

> The life of a Master today is Richard Whistler's story:

Modern tonnage has changed out of all recognition to tonnage employed in the iron ore trade of twenty years ago. Major changes have taken place in the size of the vessels, the size of the crews and the automation. In the 1990's a Britsh flag, British owned and British operated ore carrier of about 173,000 deadweight tonnes will be about 288 metres lons, 47 metres wide and have a summer draught of 17.8 metres. A crew size operating today will be about 20 persons, although the ship can be certificated to operate a crew size of sixteen. A typical engine power will be 20,000 BHP, on a speed of $13^{1}/_{2}$ knots in ballast, and $12^{1}/_{2}$ loaded. This ship could operate at an economical speed of about $10^{1}/_{2}$ knots in ballast, 10 loaded, on something like 25 tons of fuel a day.

Twenty years ago, a ship employed in similar trades as today's bulkships would have been about 10,000 tonnes deadweight, trading from the UK ports to Canadian ports like Seven Islands, for iron ore, then back to, say, Port Talbot, Workington, Irlam on the Manchester Ship Canal, or Dagenham on the River Thames. The larger bulk carriers of today will be operating from Seven Islands to Hunterston near Glasgow, Port Talbot, Immingham and Redcar. There is also another port, near Seven Islands, that was not opened twenty years ago, Port Cartier.

That ship trading to Seven islands twenty years ago would have had a crew of about thirty five. About the only thing that has not changed on these North Atlantic trips is the weather! It remains a very serious factor in the job, both for the operator, and the crews themselves, of course, with heavy rolling, much of the time at reduced speed, seas regularly coming over the decks and, in the larger ships, extreme flexing in a seaway.

The larger ships do not roll as much as the smaller ships, but rolls of up to twenty two degrees have been recorded on ships of 173,000 deadweight tonnes in the North Atlantic, and ten degrees is a pretty regular roll when the vessels are in the loaded conditions in a typical North Atlantic swell.

In the older, smaller ships, there were probably two holds which were loaded through four hatchways with iron ore, whereas, on the bigger ships of today it is standard practice to have nine holds, of which five are loaded with iron ore, which is an extremely heavy cargo. In the coal trade, which is a much lighter bulk cargo, all nine hatches are normally used.

In the coal trades, the big Cape size 100,000 tonners and over are usually employed from Richards Bay in South Africa, to Korea, Japan, the west coast of Canada to the Far East, Australia to Korea and Japan, or back to Europe. Often we load part cargo in Richards Bay for Korea and Japan. A ship engaged in this sort of trade would possibly load a part cargo of coal in Norfolk, USA, top off in Richards Bay and discharge in the Far East. She would then proceed to Australia and either load coal or iron ore for Europe. After discharging in Europe, she may be back out for another cargo of coal, or iron ore from South America, bound for the Far East, and so the cycle will continue.

Twenty years ago, it took weeks to load and discharge. Today, loading rates vary from port to port but pretty average loading rates are about 6,000 tonnes per hour. The average overall discharge rate will be something like 2,000 tonnes an hour, so the ships are not in port very long, usually about thirty hours loading and two to three days discharging. Many of these ports around the world are especially designed to handle the big ships and with enormous stockpile space are very isolated, so one has little incentive to try and get ashore because of the distance from the local towns.

This isolation gives other problems, like storing and repairs. For instance, when storing in some of these ports, one has to send the order in fairly well in advance, so that supplies can be brought in from much further afield. A classic case was ordering long life milk for a voyage across the Pacific from Prince Rupert Island in Canada, where the town itself carried very limited supplies. The order had to be sent in three or four days prior to arrival, so that they would arrive in time.

The long passages at sea today in these high-tech ships – we're talking in terms of fifty two days from the United States to the Far East via Richards Bay, and forty eight from Australia to Europe – can play havoc with maintenance schedules, with the limited amount of time in port that we have seen. Main engine maintenance can be seriously affected and may, in the end, require the ship to stop at sea with the consequences of off hire and the added costs to the shipowner or charterer.

The major reductions in crew sizes have taken place in the catering department, the engine room and the seamen employed on deck. Today's modern, large bulk carrier under the British flag will have just a cook and a steward in the catering department. The engineering department will consist of the chief and three other engineers, an electrician and two motor men. As the engine room today is unmanned during the hours of darkness, less men are needed for watchkeeping. Similarly, on deck the ships are down to a bo'sun and five men. The complement of officers in the deck department remains virtually the same as in the past, with the Master, three mates and a radio officer.

Reduction in the catering department has obviously meant a big change in operating conditions. Meals for the ratings and for the officers are usually all self service, although they have separate dining areas. There is no longer early morning tea for the officers or the plate of toast for the mate at 6.00 am as there was in the old days. The rest of the ratings are involved with cleaning the accommodation, indeed more so than in the past. The steward still carries out the tasks of making the beds and cleaning the officers' cabins, but his cleaning operations have been drastically reduced; for instance, the officers now are responsible for cleaning their own bar.

Common television rooms are the norm on board ships these days, rather than separate lounges for crew and officers. It is generally liked, although there is still the problem of who wants to watch what! Videos are supplied by the Company, and supplemented by individual crew members, so there is no shortage of films to watch on the longer passages. There is a feeling that moves are afoot to have one bar for the whole ship's company, but, generally speaking, both officers and ratings are against it, as both prefer their own bars. It is probably better that way as discipline still has to be maintained on board ship, and as all the crew are on board twenty four hours a day, officers do not want to discuss their business in front of the ratings. The same applies in reverse, of course. Although inter-bar activity takes place in the shape of darts matches, quizzes and the like, it does give people the opportunity at the end of the day to return to their respective bars. The old days of drinking in cabins and inviting friends around has died out.

With the reductions in crews there is much more automation on board ships. The engineering department is fully automated and, in general, ships have shaft generators so that the diesel alternators need not run at sea, which gives a massive saving in diesel oil consumption. Moreover, diesel engines are fitted to run on intermediate fuel (mixtures of heavy fuel and diesel), thereby cutting the costs of the fuel bill. Deck equipment includes all the mooring ropes on drums which can be controlled from one position on the fo'c'sle, or on the poop, so once the ropes are actually on the bollards ashore, one man can control the tying up of the ship, and he can also adjust the moorings as may be necessary. Side opening hatch covers are one man-operated, all cleating and opening operations being hydraulically operated.

One operation has not changed, however; indeed, it is worse on the larger ships of today. Ore- and coal-dust spillage on decks after loading and discharge has to be cleaned off the hatch covers aswell as the deck, and can take up to three days on the 170,000 tonner; if you loaded at Nouadhibou in Mauretania it can take a week. In this port the loader was built for small ships, and the only way to get the ore into the holds in the correct stow is to aim high and have a high belt speed. As the wind blows predominantly from ahead and along the full length of the ship, she is inches deep in ore dust over all the decks, and sometimes up to a foot deep between the hatch coamings. It all has to be dug and deposited in the holds, or overboard, before washing down!

On UK flag, UK crewed vessels, crews are rotated on a four to six month basis on board, with ten days leave per month served being given to ratings, and fifteen to seventeen days per officer. On non-UK flag vessels the leave varies from three days per month served, for all ranks, to ten to fifteen days for officers, with time on board usually longer than on UK flagged ships. In some cases it is very much longer. Crews are generally changed on UK flagged vessels in small batches, thereby maintaining continuity on board, so that, if the ship rarely comes back to the UK, the ships company does quite a lot of flying each year, and each ship's staff are experts on one liners to describe airlines and airports throughout the world! Economy class, of course, for all ranks.

The Wake of the Cachalots

JOHN NOBLE: GOING ASHORE

The companies that sustain Britain's merchant marine today have survived only by dramatic evolution. Ships that could not make a profit have mostly been scrapped, and a lack of incentive to invest in the merchant fleet has precluded new orders; where the ships could not make a living with crews receiving European rates of pay, they have been flagged out. Some companies turned to ship management as either their main marine occupation or as a fringe operation, and this has often been where large fleet reductions have been made, releasing management expertise without losing that expertise from the company. Many companies, of course, have diversified into non-shipping activities, with long-term plans that leave the marine sector far behind them.

But what of the British Master Mariner in all this, what future does he have under the disappearing Red Duster? The answer is, he must evolve, and for John Noble, that has meant carving out a new career ashore.

John Noble completed his indentures with the old and respected company of Alfred Holt, the Blue Funnel Line of Liverpool. After a period of service with a number of companies, in 1970 John joined Palm Line Limited as Third Officer. The Palm Line was one of the leading companies serving West Africa, with a tradition of fine vessels built to their own specification with the West African trade in mind. When John joined them, they had a fleet of sixteen vessels ranging from 7,000 to 13,000 gross tons, and he served with them through to the rank of Chief Officer. After obtaining his Master's Certificate, he saw that the future lay ashore and studied at Southampton University and the College of Nautical Studies at Warsash where he obtained a Batchelor of

Science degree in nautical studies. After working for some time with a British Protection and Indemnity club, specialising in marine insurance, John returned to Warsash to lecture. In 1980, he opened the London office of Murray Fenton & Associates, marine and cargo surveyors, and over the past twelve years John's experience in the surveying world has been wide as he developed a speciality in salvage, wreck removal and oil pollution. John joined the Southampton Master Mariners Club almost immediately after gaining his Masters Ticket and was Captain of the Club in 1989. Here he gives us a lively account of a Cachalot who goes ashore.

"Morning Captain."

"Who are you?"

"I'm the surveyor appointed by your owners to protect the ship's interests."

This normal introduction between surveyor and shipmaster will be the start of a relationship which may end years later in Court or Arbitration when the issues, which required the surveyor's attendance in the first palce, are sometimes resolved. Over the past ten years I have conducted surveys and associated work in over 35 countries worldwide. The range of assignments has been enormous, from major salvage incidents involving fully-laden VLCC's to examining twenty foot containers! To succeed as an international surveyor, technical expertise is a must, but just as important is the ability to get on with people. Also needed is infinite patience aswell as integrity, a sense of humour, tact, diplomacy and a strong stomach! At Murray Fenton we have acted for shipowners, charterers, cargo owners, berth operators, brokers, Government agencies and the European Commission to name but a few.

Any surveyor is only as good as his last survey. Mistakes, or errors in judgment may be forgiven, but a breach of integrity never will. A client must have complete trust in 'his' surveyor. There are times when client relations become difficult when, having acted for him on one occasion, he finds the same surveyor acting for 'the other side' on a different case. Promises of holidays on yachts, villas in the sun or even brown envelopes must be politely but firmly rejected. 'First come, first served' must be the rule to maintain independence.

It's a funny old job, which takes you all over the world. International travel is interesting, and challenging! Often the most difficult part of any job is getting there in one piece. I find airports fascinating places, where the inevitable delays give an opportunity to study one's fellow beings. I have seen family rows develop, explode and die down over trivial items such as who is going to take little Johnny to the loo! Tearful farewells and joyous reunions all take place at airports. Sometimes one adopts or is adopted by a fellow passenger; I remember assisting a dear elderly lady at check-in with her clearly overweight suitcase. After taking her around the duty-free shop (and inevitably pushing her trolley) I listened to her family history while waiting to board. The conversation – or, rather, monologue – continued while we waited for our luggage at the destination and I was introduced to her welcoming party as "That nice man from London". Only after ritual hugs, kisses and bone-crushing handshakes could I make a decent withdrawal.

The most infuriating aspect of travelling is the delay caused by having to comply with visa requirements. In some situations, the response to an urgent shipping casualty is delayed while I await the wheels of bureaucracy to turn. The common factor which seems to unite countries in the world is the attitude of officials at airports. Many appear to take some perverse pleasure in seeing a long queue of tired, perspiring travellers awaiting their attention. One of the biggest uncertainties is whether or not to offer a bribe. There is a common misconception that officials practically everywhere require 'inducements' to ease the rigors of formality. Not so – a golden rule is never to offer money unsolicited; the penalties for 'corrupting' officials is often severe.

There is no glamour in modern air travel; flying is an unnatural experience and the hassle of continual queuing for check-in, immigration, customs, boarding, even going to the loo, is just tiresome. The one consolation of modern flight conveniences is that the in-flight movie usually sends me to sleep!

If one must spend many nights every year in hotels, creature comforts take on increased importance. To say it is possible to judge a bar or restaurant by the state of its toilets is all too true internationally. The worst hotel in which I have stayed was in Algeria; the filth in the bathroom literally induced retching, bedlinen was unwashed and damp and the food defied description. The presence of rats and cockroaches is so commonplace (even in the United States) that they are barely worth a mention!

One particular chain of hotels is well-known for its ladies of the night. The temptation, however, is easy to resist, particlarly now with AIDS. The most embarrassing experience which I encountered was in Singapore. I had just arrived after a sixteen hour flight and turned in. I was barely asleep when the telephone rang and a female voice said, "It's me, I'm on my way up." Panic set in; I hadn't been in Singapore for twenty years, was my past catching up with me? There was a knock at the door, but, looking through the peephole, all I could see was the top of a head. Knock knock, again and again. In order to avoid disturbing the other guests, I opened the door and standing there was a truly beautiful Chinese girl. "How do I get out of this?" I asked myself. My ego was quickly deflated when my visitor then said with surprise, "It's not you". My visitor, who I later discovered was the hotel pianist, explained that she had arranged to meet an Australian in his room after she finished work. What she had not known was that he had evidently checked out (or changed rooms, I suppose) and I had been given his old room. The girl had arrived with a bottle of wine and a bouquet of flowers; it must have been love! Suffice to say, she left immediately, leaving the flowers and taking the wine.

In the same vein, but with more sinister implications, was an experience which I had in Lagos. After a long, hot and tiring day I returned to the hotel to find, as usual, no water. I then repaired to the open air pool bar for a welcome Star beer. As happens when in some of the less welcoming parts of the world, I engaged in conversation with another resident who was in Nigeria dealing with some project. Gradually, the circle grew and horror tales of travel were exchanged, hotel stories abounded and the supply of Star was plentiful. I took no notice of the two or three dusky maidens who hovered on the edge of the circle; there was no doubt as to their inclinations, but I had assumed that they were with someone.

By the time that the water supply was back on, it was late. I signed my share of the bill, confirming the room number by showing my key, as is often the custom. I then retired to my room, wrote up my notes for the day and prepared for bed. The room was not air conditioned, so in order to catch the breeze it was necessary to open the window and leave the door ajar, but on the chain. It is usual to set booby traps in the room so that if entry is gained there is warning. I had set up a chain of obstacles, such as glasses balanced on the edge of the metal waste bin, drawing pins on the floor and so on, to deter entry – or at least alert me.

I was awoken sometime later by one of my makeshift intruder alarms, when a glass, balanced on the door, fell and smashed. I saw a hand clawing around the door trying to undo the security chain. A short, Anglo-Saxon exchange followed, when I discovered that one of the dusky bar maidens was trying to get in. "Let me in – let me in – you promised." Rather bemused, I denied making any such promises and told the intruder to be off! I underestimated the persistence of the lady, who, on finding that I would not be an easy touch, then resorted to creating a scene. What a din! She shouted, kicked the door and screamed – even after I forced the door shut. The whole floor must have been roused. I suppose she thought that I would be embarrassed into letting her in.

When I mentioned the incident to others the following evening, apart from being the centre of ribald comment, I was advised that this ruse was used often and the lady was one of a gang of room robbers, who, having gained entry and plundered, relied on the victims' embarrassment at falling into the 'honey trap' to get away with it!

In our business, hotels are not judged on superficial items such as comfort, food and efficiency alone. The key to conducting an assignment successfully is good communication: reliable telephones, telex and Fax machines are as essential in an hotel as any other amenity. Hotel costs have soared and generally, value for money is poor. There are a number of 'rip-off' tactics used by hotels, the worst of which is in Hong Kong. Most, if not all European flights leave Hong Kong between 8 pm and 11 pm. A half day supplement is charged until 6 pm and if check-out is after 6 pm, the room is charged for a whole day. You might check in at, say, 11 pm one day and check out at 7 pm the next day, and be charged 2 days for a 20 hour stay.

A surveyor travelling abroad must be self-reliant. Often as not, there is nobody to meet you at the airport. Finding the hotel or Agent's office can be difficult, particularly in those countries where English is not commonly spoken. The longest land journey I have undertaken was in Sudan, when no internal flights were available and I had to endure a 17 hour bus journey from Khartoum to Port Sudan. The natural stops at roadside facilities were a real eye-opener; interesting, but not an experience to be repeated.

The most hair raising taxi journey took place in Brazil when I went from Rio to Sao Sabasto on the coast road. The driver was quite mad; we only left the road once, but I spent much of the time lying across the back seat. I still do not know what side of the road the Brazilians drive on!

In many countries the commercial port facilities are considered security areas and in order to gain access a port pass is essential. Sometimes this involves a simple procedure and the delay is simply irritating, but in certain countries it can take days. I have been interviewed by secret police on a number of occasions and have lost count of the number of searches I have gone through when entering or leaving port areas. Nothing is achieved by reacting to the often ill-mannered or sadistic approach used by so many officials; the easiest way through is to grin and bear it. Like many, I do not feel comfortable if I have to give up my passport, a requirement in many ports. On one job, I found a use for my British Rail season ticket card. Instead of offering my passport I jokingly offered the British Rail card, only to find it was accepted!

The physical act of boarding the ship is often the most hazardous part of the job, even in port. Gangway safety is often abysmal, but no one is going to pay a surveyor to stand on the quay! Boarding a grounded ship can be difficult and dangerous. On one casualty off Bermuda, the ship was heading right into the prevailing weather, and a conventional pilot ladder boarding at the ship's side was impossible. A Jacob's ladder was rigged over the stern and careful judgment was needed in the fifteen foot seas to step from the boat to the ladder. The boatman in charge, Herbie Adderley, was superb and over two hundred boat transfers were made without incident. Indeed, the skills of a boatman are a vital ingredient in safe boarding. I recall another occasion, when, trying to board a wreck, we found ourselves on the wrong side of the surf line at the foot of some sheer cliffs near Cape Finisterre. It was too late to criticise the helmsman; a strong sense of self-preservation, a loud voice and responsive outboard engines resulted in safety being reached after my 'taking over' and powering the rubber boat through the surf, much to the relief of those watching from the shore as they had been on the verge of calling up the helicopter which was standing by near the scene!

Aboard at last, the first formality for any surveyor must be to advise the Master of his presence. Apart from common courtesy, ship's staff must know who is aboard and where, for safety reasons. This courtesy is often overlooked by attending surveyors. Sometimes they are trying to be cute and catch the captain unawares, but often they do not know or appreciate their position while on board.

Many surveyors are quite straightforward; establishing the nature, cause and extent of cargo damage requires experience, powers of observation and knowledge of the commodity being examined. The fun really starts when trying to reach agreement on site as to the scale of the problem. As a visiting surveyor in foreign ports, I have been given an opportunity to see how others reach a conclusion. For example, I surveyed a cargo of maize that had become badly water damaged as a result of water ingress through hatch covers. There were columns of hot, rotting maize and large, vertical 'V' wedges of damaged maize where water had persistently entered through the cross joins. It was quite straightforward to estimate the volume of damage by looking at the damage pattern in the cargo. At a meeting, held to try to reach agreement between surveyors as to the extent of the damage, the local clique turned fact into fantasy and proposed a horizontal layer theory, this took the form of, say, a two metre layer 100% damaged; three metre layer 50%; two metre layer 25% and so on. Needless to say, the total damage estimated by this arbitrary method greatly exceeded the actual damage and bore no relation to the damage pattern observed. Of the six or more surveyors attending, not one had entered the holds to estimate!

Often the issues surrounding a shipping casualty are complex, especially where there is pollution, or the threat of it. I have attended many serious casualties where oil or chemical pollution has been a major factor. In each instance I have had deep involvement with local authorities, and it may come as a surprise, but full co-operation is not always forthcoming. Consider a case where an unladen VLCC was aground, but still with hundreds of tons of fuel oil aboard, broached-to and in great danger of breaking up. A salvage team flew in essential salvage and pollution control equipment which had to be in place desperately quickly, only to have the equipment impounded for twenty four hours while customs formalities were completed.

At other times it is difficult to convince Authorities that everything is being done to deal with a situation, particularly where a casualty is located in a sensitive position. Equipment mobilisation takes time and during this period the casualty situation can change. This can be a tense period because the surveyor becomes the whipping boy for the Authorities' frustration. The advice that we generally give to principals is, "Do something"; for example, an oil containment boom can often be placed, even if it is of limited effect.

A casualty becomes a wreck when hull and machinery underwriters have paid out on an actual or constructive total loss, when the liability for its removal may lie with the shipowner and, consequentially, his P and I club. In these circumstances liability only attaches if the State, in whose waters the wreck lies, has in its statutes a provision that makes the removal of the wreck the owner's liability. It is surprising, though, how many countries do not have this statutory provision. Problems then arise when the attending surveyor has to tell the Authority that the owner (or his club) will not remove the offending and often unsightly wreck. I attended one case where a state had no wreck removal provisions on their statute books and the Authorities were so put out, that they tried to invoke the anti-litter provisions in its laws!

Each casualty is different and generates a life of its own. The relationship between interested parties forms an integral component of response development. Petty wrangling and personality clashes are the most common sources of irritation. Once a job turns sour, it is difficult, if not impossible, to retrieve the situation. The simplest analogy is to think of cargo stowage; when loading starts, it is essential to ensure a tight, good stow, or else the consequences will be disastrous as cargo loading and stowage progresses.

There are no golden rules in dealing with serious casualties; the circumstances of the incident will dictate how an investigation or response will develop. Perhaps it is cynical to mention the point, but very often all is not what it seems. Questions raised can be, for example:

"Was the chart now on board the one in use at the time?"

"Is the log book a factual account of what did occur, or has it been completed with the benefit of hindsight?"

"Who was on the bridge at the time?"

"Am I really expected to believe this?"

There has been a tendency to rebuild the facts of an incident in order to hide the truth and sometimes the efforts are clumsy or misguided, resulting in the situation becoming worse for the perpetrator of the fabrication than it might otherwise have been! The ability to develop a 'nose' for a case is as important an attribute as technical knowledge. I constantly have to remind myself that we see ships only when there is trouble; thousands of voyages are completed without incident.

It is difficult to single out one assignment as being the most unusual. As part of follow-up work, I have ended up miles from the sea: a tractor factory inland in the United States; the Iranian Embassy in Ankara; a food processing factory in Banbury and a naval headquarters two hundred miles from the sea at an altitude of ten thousand feet in Quito, Ecuador, are but a few of the unusual locations that I have visited. The most tense assignment took place in Bermuda when a fully laden, 200,000 tonnes VLCC ran aground on the reef. The potential for a catastrophic pollution was immense, but luckily the ship was refloated just as the swell preceding a hurricane was starting to build up. Within hours, conditions were atrocious and it is certain that some or all of the tanks would have ruptured had the ship remained aground. The sigh of relief from the tourist board and other authorities could be heard above the noise of hurricane force winds! We have weighed Blackfriars Railway Bridge as it was being dismantled, inspected a damaged helicopter, counted rice weevils in samples, drilled holes in semi-solid, wet sugar, inspected jetfoils and given lectures in Amman, all in the line of duty.

One of the most challenging aspects of consultancy is involvement in the litigation process. Sometimes we are asked to provide expert assistance on particular topics; occasionally, cases in which we have been involved in the field, end up in Court or Arbitration. Giving oral evidence in support of a report and being cross-examined is an interesting experience, about as enjoyable as sitting Masters orals! I have given evidence on unsafe port issues, log carrying from West Africa, cargo gear, contingency planning and hatch covers, to name but a few topics.

I have given evidence in courts not only in the UK but also around the world. The old Dubai Court House was located in the Fort. The hearing took place in a judge's chambers (his office) and was informal but fair. Of greater interest was the activity in the square, where actual or alleged felons were dragged to and fro. Just inside the entrance was a cage where, I presumed, those awaiting trial were kept.

The contrast between a court appearance in Sweden, where everything was orderly and organised, and in Sudan, where the court building hummed with seemingly constant and chaotic activity, was acute. It would be easy to conclude that the hustle and bustle in Port Sudan meant that a similar approach might be taken in the court room. Suffice to say, that I conducted an on-board survey on the Saturday and Sunday, prepared the report on Monday, presented it on Tuesday and gave evidence, with cross examination on Wednesday. The hearing was conducted in Arabic, with a translation by an interpreter. Each of my answers was recorded in Arabic, Counsel on each side having to agree that the translation was correct before it was written down. I was impressed, and so was the London based solicitor who was travelling with me.

It would be easy to fill endless pages with tales from afar, but I suppose that I must close somewhere. Looking towards home, a company such as mine, Murray Fenton, relies upon the goodwill and competence of its staff. I can be called out at any time, often to travel abroad for an unspecified duration at short notice. The office must still run smoothly and deal with crises that all offices face, without me. I do the work at the sharp end, but the final product, the report, must be typed, proof-read and bound by my staff, while batting a hundred and one other matters. Thanks to all of you.

The Wake of the Cachalots

'FINISHED WITH ENGINES'

The British Merchant Navy was a child of our imperial expansion, whose halcyon period was the mid-nineteenth century when Britain and her Empire became established as the workshop of the world. The Empire was an economic one, infinitely more than it ever claimed to be a military one. In order to flourish, the Empire needed a safe and reliable sea transport system, for the safe passage of passengers, cargoes and mails. To secure this system, British businessmen established not only their shipping companies but also those things upon which their businesses depended: bunkering stations, ship repair facilities and agents. The whole was governed by maritime law and protected by the Royal Navy.

The sun set on the Empire some forty years ago, and as British shipowners found themselves unable to compete with unprotected trades and the low wage-cost ships operated by Far East and Third World countries, the Red Duster fell from the favour of successive British governments, so that, without a champion to fight for its cause, it could not have hoped to flourish in the modern economics of shipping, and has all but disappeared, giving way to flags of convenience and cheaper competiton. If it is to have a future at all, British shipping now must find it in the European Economic Community.

The Cachalots are men who have had to command by personality; they have seen enormous changes in their careers and one cannot escape the fact that the seafarer has been responsible for the prosperity of the country's balance sheet. It should also be remembered that he has secured our survival and Bacon's words are as vital today as ever:

"He that commands the sea is at great liberty and may take as much and as little of the war as he will."

Seafaring is what we know best in these British Isles; we have had to rely on it for hundreds of years and we have become extremely good at it.

But what of the future? The captains of Britain's industry today see our future very clearly in a Europe of equal, united partners, where we all have our own particular contributions to make, and there can be no doubt that our expertise in shipping and seafaring is the greatest contibution that we can make to the future prosperity of the European Economic Community. The sea is the essence of Britain's heritage and the Cachalots have earned their distinction as the lynchpin in this national asset which is as vital to us today as ever: 98% by weight of all our trade still travels by sea. Surely it is madness to abandon your most vital asset?